MW01032567

10,00
1—7

Dream and Existence

HAVER,

MICHEL FOUCAULT AND LUDWIG BINSWANGER

Dream and Existence

Translated by

Forrest Williams and Jacob Needleman

A Special Issue from the

Review of Existential Psychology & Psychiatry

Edited by Keith Hoeller

Vol. XIX   No. 1

Preparation of this book was aided by a grant from the Publications Program of the National Endowment for the Humanities, an independent federal agency.

© Copyright 1986 by Keith Hoeller

Review of Existential Psychology & Psychiatry

Vol. XIX, no. 1   1984-85

DREAM AND EXISTENCE

Editor's Foreword

KEITH HOELLER

I belong to that generation who as students had before their eyes, and were limited by, a horizon consisting of Marxism, phenomenology, and existentialism . . . at the time I was working on my book about the history of madness [*Madness & Civilization*]. I was divided between existential psychology and phenomenology, and my research was an attempt to discover the extent these could be defined in historical terms.[1]

Michel Foucault
September, 1984

While the names of Michel Foucault and Ludwig Binswanger are familiar to the readers of the *Review of Existential Psychology & Psychiatry*, the linking of their names together as co-authors of a single volume is likely to come as a surprise—not only to you—but to many others as well. Naturally, the Binswanger pole of the conjunction needs little explanation. Binswanger was of course a pioneer Swiss psychiatrist in existential analysis (*Daseinsanalyse*), colleague of Sigmund Freud and Martin Heidegger, and author of the first work in existential psychiatry to be written under the influence of Heidegger's *Being and Time*: (1927):[2] "Dream and Existence" (1930).[3]

But with Michel Foucault it is another matter. It is true of course that the first of his books to appear in English, *Madness and Civilization*,[4] was published in R. D. Laing's series, *Studies in Existentialism and Phenomenology*, with an Introduction by David Cooper, inventor of the term "anti-psychiatry." Foucault's book originally appeared in 1961, an important year for existential psychiatry and other alternatives to traditional psychiatric approaches. Both Thomas Szasz' *The Myth of Mental Illness*[5] and Laing's *Self and Others*[6] were published in 1961. In this same year, the *Review of Existential Psychology & Psychiatry* published its first volume, which included essays by Viktor Frankl, Paul Tillich, Rollo May, Adrian Van Kaam, F. J. Buytendijk, Leslie Farber, and Carl Rogers. Given this fertile intellectual climate, it is not at all surprising that Laing and Cooper should find a kindred spirit in Foucault and his "history of madness," as is evidenced by the following passage from Cooper's Introduction:

Recent psychiatric—or perhaps anti-psychiatric—research into the origins of the major form of madness in our age, schizophrenia, has moved round to the position that people do not in fact go mad, but are driven mad by others who are driven into the position of driving them mad by a peculiar convergence of social pressures. The social pressures, hinted at by Foucault, are mediated to certain selected individuals by their families— themselves selected by processes that are intelligible—through various mystifying and confusing maneuvers.[7]

7

Certainly, what Foucault's book has in common with the thought of Laing and Cooper, or for that matter, even with Szasz' approach, is that so-called "mental illness" is not understood as an isolated, intrapsychic entity existing merely within the individual patient. Rather, in order to write the history of madness, one must put the patient back into a world again and write the history of madmen *and* society, patients *and* doctors. In other words, what all these critics of psychiatry have in common is the Heideggerean notion that human beings are always constituted by the concept of "being-in-the-world," and that "madness" is a societal event which occurs *between* people who may in fact have conflicting values and goals. As Foucault makes clear in his Preface to *Madness and Civilization*, it is his purpose to return to the original schism between madness and society:

> None of the concepts of psychopathology, even and especially in the implicit process of retrospections, can play an organizing role. What is constitutive is the action that divides madness, and not the science elaborated once this division is made and calm restored . . . As for a common language, there is no such thing; or rather, there is no such thing any longer; the constitution of madness as a mental illness, at the end of the eighteenth century, affords the evidence of a broken dialogue, posits the separation as already effected, and thrusts into oblivion all those stammered, imperfect words without fixed syntax in which the exchange between madness and reason was made. The language of psychiatry, which is a monologue of reason *about* madness, has been established only on the basis of such a silence. I have not tried to write the history of that language, but rather the archaeology of that silence.[8]

Precisely what Foucault is concerned with is what he will later call, "a *historical knowledge of struggles*."[9] In a 1977 interview, he says,

> When I was studying during the early 1950's, one of the great problems that arose was that of the political status of science and the ideological functions which it could serve . . . . These [problems] can all be summed up in two words: power and knowledge. I believe I wrote *Madness & Civilization* to some extent within the horizon of these questions.[10]

These questions of power and knowledge, and the political status of psychiatry as a science, are all questions which Foucault shares in common with the existential psychiatrists and with Szasz. However, *Madness and Civilization*, Foucault's doctoral thesis, does not explicitly invoke existentialism and phenomenology, and certainly does not abound with references to Kierkegaard, Husserl, Heidegger, Merleau-Ponty, and Sartre. One finds only passing reference to the German poet, Friedrich Hölderlin, about whom Heidegger has written so much, and to Nietzsche. This is in spite of the fact that, as Foucault himself has admitted in the interview cited at the beginning of this Foreword, he was steeped in the tradition of existentialism and phenomenology.[11] This is even more surprising when one realizes that there is a stage in Foucault's intellectual development, indeed, the very first stage, in which existential and phenomenological psychiatry are explicitly invoked to characterize his work. This stage in the development of his thought has remained relatively unknown. While the studies by Sheridan[12] and Dreyfus and Rabinow[13] notably refer to this early stage in their Introductions, like most works on Foucault, they begin their commentaries in earnest with *Madness and Civilization*.

This stage is characterized by Foucault's first two published works: "Dream, Imagination, and Existence" and *Mental Illness and Psychology*.[14] Both of these works appeared in 1954, and both can be characterized as studies in existential psychiatry. Foucault's first book, for example, *Mental Illness and Psychology*, claims "phenomenological psychology" as the method for understanding "mental illness," and quotes Jaspers, Minkowski, Heidegger, and Binswanger. In the culminating chapter of the first part of the book, which, echoing Binswanger's essay "Dream and Existence," is entitled "Mental Illness and Existence," Foucault writes:

> The understanding of the sick consciousness and the reconstitution of its pathological world, these are the two tasks of a phenomenology of mental illness.[15]

This book, which was originally published in 1954, and which was substantially revised for a second edition in 1962, concludes with a second part. In this second part, published in 1962, Foucault explicitly states the results of *Madness and Civilization*, and indeed the words express a conclusion in agreement with Szasz' work, *The Myth of Mental Illness*:[16]

> The preceding analyses have fixed the coordinates by which psychologies can situate the pathological fact. But although they showed the forms of appearance of the illness, they have been unable to show its conditions of appearance. It would be a mistake to believe that organic evolution, psychological history, or the situation of man in the world may reveal these conditions....But the roots of the pathological deviation, as such, are to be found elsewhere....mental illness has its reality and its value qua illness only within a culture that recognizes it as such....The analyses of our psychologists and sociologists, which turn the patient into a deviant and which seek the origin of the morbid in the abnormal, are, therefore, above all a projection of culture themes.[17]

In other words, "mental illness" is not in fact an "illness" like any other; rather, it is a relation between self and other:

> When a doctor thinks he is diagnosing madness as a phenomenon of nature, it is the existence of this threshold that enables him to make such a judgment....But there is nothing to compel a diagnosis of "mental" illness....I have purposefully not referred to the physiological and

anatomicopathological problems concerning mental illness...neither psychology nor therapeutics can become those absolute viewpoints from which the psychology of mental illness can be reduced or suppressed.[18]

The titles of the two parts of the 1962 version of *Mental Illness and Psychology* bear out the evolution in Foucault's viewpoint from 1954 to 1961. The first part (1954), in which phenomenological psychology is put to work, is entitled "The Psychological Dimensions of Mental Illness," while the second part (1962) is called "Madness and Culture." The movement is one from a concentration on the world of the individual subject, on the history of the individual, to a focus on the subject's relation to society and the relation between madness and civilization historically. In other words, one cannot study the individual's history alone and reach any valid conclusions. One must situate the individual historically and societally:

> In fact, it is only in history that one can discover the sole concrete *a priori* from which mental illness draws, with the empty opening up of its possibility, its necessary figures.[19]

Thus the need for an historical account of madness such as *Madness and Civilization*.

In the 1984 interview in which Foucault indicates his being torn between existential psychology and phenomenology while writing *Madness and Civilization*, he says "my research was an attempt to discover the extent these could be defined in historical terms."[20] He goes on to immediately say, "That's when I discovered that the subject would have to be defined in other terms than Marxism or phenomenology."[21] All of this would seem to indicate that in Foucault's discovery of the importance of history, he felt that phenomenology concentrated on the individual subject and could not lead him over to a historical determination of the role of madness, which would explain why *Madness and Civilization* does not explicitly invoke phenomenology or the phenomenologists. That Foucault holds this view of phenomenology is further confirmed by a 1977 interview on "Truth and Power," where he says:

> But this historical contextualization needed to be something more than the simple relativisation of the phenomenological subject. I don't believe the problem can be solved by historicizing the subject as posited by the phenomenologists, fabricating a subject that evolves through the course of history. One has to dispense with the constituent subject, to get rid of the subject itself, that's to say, to arrive at an analysis which can account for the constitution of the subject within a historical framework. And this is what I would call genealogy, that is, a form of history which can account for the constitution of knowledges, discourses, domains of objects, etc., without having to make reference to a subject which is

either transcendental in relation to the field of events or runs in its empty
sameness throughout the course of history.[22]

This quotation gives rise to an obvious question: When Foucault links
phenomenology to the subject, in particular to a constituent, transcendental, almost ahistorical subject, precisely whose phenomenology does he
have in mind? It is clear that it could not be Heidegger's version of
phenomenology, since it was the central task of *Being and Time* to dispense
with the "subject" and to ground *Dasein* in a historical world. I also do
not think it would apply to Boss' conception of Daseinsanalysis, which
follows Heidegger rather closely. And clearly Laing and Cooper had no
difficulty in recognizing the importance of the historical aspect of madness
in society. I would submit that the above quotation sounds like Foucault
still retained a rather Husserlian notion of phenomenology and
phenomenological psychology, which did not get beyond Husserl's
phenomenological reduction. Let me just sight one passage from Husserl's
Phenomenological Psychology:

> And the phenomenological epoché "switches" this off in its entirety—
> therefore also personal mentality in its existence in the natural world. It
> reduces all that to its phenomenality and takes its own position not in the
> world, but in the subjectivity....The disclosure of pure subjectivity: the
> actual execution of the indications begun in the lecture would include the
> entire doctrine of constitution, but resting on that and gradually becoming
> detached from it, a universal doctrine of the structures of individual
> subjectity and intersubjectivity.[23]

To be sure, even for Husserl there was to be a transition to intersubjectivity
and from a psychological to a transcendental-phenomenological reduction:
"the fundamental science then becomes transcendental phenomenology,
a *psychology* of the highest sense, a new sense which includes all critique
of reason and all genuine philosophical problems."[24] How successful Husserl was at making this transition is still being debated.

One thing is clear, however: phenomenological psychology, as conceived by Husserl, brackets out all the things that Foucault wants to
include, such as power and history. While it is true that Foucault knew
Husserl's thought well, how is it nevertheless possible that, after having
studied Binswanger so thoroughly, he could still retain a Husserlian notion
of phenomenological psychology? After all, Binswanger was the first to
attempt to found a psychology on Heidegger's philosophy.

I think the answer lies in the philosophically ambivalent nature of
the Binswangerian enterprise. In a masterful essay entitled, "Ludwig
Binswanger and the Sublimation of the Self," the literary critic Paul de
Man argues that Binswanger is confronted with a problem when he attempts
to apply ontological insights to a particular ontic case:

> A certain degree of confusion arises when this knowledge is interpreted
> as a *means* to act upon the destiny that the knowledge reveals. This is
> the moment at which the ontological inquiry is abandoned for empirical
> concerns that are bound to lead it astray.[25]

De Man goes on to say that Binswanger is most at home with the description
of individual clinical cases, and even his more general attempts to outline
such ontological dimensions as "falling" remain less substantial than, for
example, Heidegger's discussions. This shows itself especially in cases
involving artists and the role of the imagination:

> [Binswanger] sees the imagination as an act of the individual will that
> remains determined, in its deepest intent, by a transcendental moment
> that lies beyond our own volition; in this, he stays within the main tradition
> of the leading theories of the imagination. But he fails to pursue the
> philosophical consequences of his insight and falls back upon a normative
> precept favoring a harmonious relationship between extension and depth
> as a necessary condition for a well-balanced personality. In the last
> analysis, as a good psychiatrist, what interests Binswanger most is the
> achievement of balance, not the truth of the fall.[26]

De Man goes on to caution that this should not necessarily be taken
as a criticism, but rather as an indication of a general problem with the
ontic-ontological relationship. De Man cites the following passage from
Foucault's *The Order of Things*, in order to point out that Foucault himself
was quite conscious of this dilemma:

> Phenomenology, although it originated first of all in a climate of anti-
> psychologism…has never been able to free itself from its tempting and
> threatening proximity to the empirical study of man. Therefore, although
> it starts out as a reduction to the *cogito*, it has always been led to ask
> questions, to ask the ontological question. We can see the phenomenolog-
> ical project dissolve under our very eyes into a description of actual
> experience that is empirical in spite of itself, and into an ontology of
> what lies beyond thought and thus bypasses the assumed primacy of the
> *cogito*.[27]

De Man himself answers the question as to precisely whose idea of
phenomenology Foucault may be thinking of here:

> This could very well have been written with Binswanger in mind, but it
> does not apply to either Husserl or Heidegger, both of whom include this
> very danger among the constituents of their philosophical insight. Foucault
> himself owes his awareness of the problem to his grounding in
> phenomenology.[28]

De Man concludes his essay by remarking that the relation of the ontic to the ontological remains a problem for contemporary literary criticism as well, which has "a tendency to forsake the barren world of ontological reduction for the wealth of lived experience."[29]

Although Binswanger was the first to directly apply Heidegger's thought to the practice of existential psychiatry, his faithfulness to Heidegger's enterprise has been called into question even by Heidegger himself. Spiegelberg puts it this way:

> For Binswanger, Heidegger had simply added another dimension to Husserl's phenomenology, in fact one which now enabled him to develop his own anthropology as the basis for what he was to call *Daseinsanalyse*. Binswanger himself admitted later that his interpretation and utilization of Heidegger's enterprise for a new anthropology was based on a misunderstanding but, in fact, a "productive," misunderstanding…of Heidegger's *Daseinsanalytik*, the attempt to use the ontological structure of human existence as the privileged access to an interpretation of the meaning of Being as such.[30]

The result has been a "phenomenological anthropology" that, while influenced by Heidegger remains perhaps more indebted to Husserl, and ultimately remains an entirely Binswangerian project.

As should now be clear, it is this Binswangerian version of psychiatry that the early Foucault of 1954 equates with phenomenological psychology in general. And it is this notion of phenomenological psychology that Foucault felt compelled to go beyond. Between 1954, when "Dream, Imagination, and Existence" was first published, and 1961, when *Madness and Civilization* appeared, there was clearly a turn in Foucault's thought. It marked a turn from the concrete, subjective world of the individual—and the preconditions for such a world—to a broader historical and political analysis of such preconditions.

*

On its own terms, Binswanger's essay "Dream and Existence" is a groundbreaking work in existential psychiatry. Published three years after Heidegger's *Being and Time*, its very first paragraph raises three concepts central to Heidegger's major work: existence, world, and Dasein. The focus on existence clearly places the piece within the existential tradition from Kierkegaard onward. The quote from Kierkegaard at the beginning of the essay makes this explicit: "Above all, we must keep in mind what it means to be a human being."[31] The quotation is from the important section in the *Concluding Unscientific Postscript*: "The Subjective Truth, Inwardness; Truth is Subjectivity." Arguing against a Hegelian view of truth as objective and rational, Kierkegaard relates knowledge back to the existing individual:

> All knowledge relates to existence, or only such knowledge as has an
> essential relationship to existence is essential knowledge...knowledge has
> a relationship to the knower, who is essentially an existing individual.[32]

It was Kierkegaard's task to remind us that as human beings we exist:
"My principal thought was that in our age, because of the great increase
of knowledge, we had forgotten what it means to *exist*, and what inwardness
signifies...."[33] He argues for a "subjective reflection," using an "indirect
method," which is based upon experience. He traces this method back to
Socrates:

> In the principle that subjectivity, inwardness, is the truth, there is com-
> prehended the Socratic wisdom, whose everlasting merit was to have
> become aware of the essential significance of existence, of the fact that
> the knower is an existing individual.[34]

Kierkegaard's subjective reflection leads to inwardness, which "culminates
in passion."[35]

Heidegger's *Being and Time* is obviously indebted to Kierkegaard.
Heidegger's question is the meaning of Being. The basic presupposition
is that rather than having a fixed essence, human beings first exist and
then decide their destinies. The ultimate knowledge comes through the
anxiety of facing the fact that we will die, and this insight is gained only
by the individual and only through a mood (*Befindlichkeit*) called dread
(*Angst*).

In order for Heidegger to inquire into the meaning of Being, he must
first lay bare the existence of the questioner, in this case *Dasein*, the name
Heidegger gives to human beings and their particular way of existing, in
order to avoid the usual philosophical problems of talking in terms of a
subject as opposed to an object. Using the phenomenological method,
which like Kierkegaard's method is descriptive, experiential, and indirect,
Heidegger discovers that the basic state of Dasein is "Being-in-the-world."
And that this Being-in-the-world is characterized by a relationship of
"care."

Following Kierkegaard and Heidegger, Binswanger's "Dream and
Existence"[36] seeks to lay bare the existing individual by concentrating on
the dream as a definite mode of human being:

> The individual's images, his feelings, his mood belong to him alone, he
> lives completely in his own world; and being completely alone means,
> psychologically speaking, dreaming.[37]

Thus, to get at the truth of the individual, means surpassing Hegel, "As psychotherapists, however, we must go beyond Hegel, for we are not dealing with *objective* truth, with the congruence between thinking and Being, but with "subjective truth," as Kierkegaard would say." We are dealing with the "passion of inwardness...."[38]

Because we first exist, and only later decide who we are and who we will become, it is not a matter, even in dreaming, of Freudian instincts which in some form determine us, since "no one has yet succeeded and no one will ever succeed in deriving the human spirit from instincts." Rather,

> An individual turns from mere self-identity to becoming a self or "the" individual, and the dreamer awakens in that unfathomable moment when he decides not only to seek to know "what hit him," but seeks also to strive into and take hold of the dynamics in these events, "himself"—the moment, that is, when he resolves to bring continuity or consequence into a life that rises and falls, falls and rises. Only then does he *make* something. That which he makes...is history.[39]

*

The *Review of Existential Psychology & Psychiatry* is extremely proud to be able to present the first English translation of Michel Foucault's very first published work, "Dream, Imagination, and Existence," together with the English translation of Ludwig Binswanger's pioneer essay in existential psychiatry, "Dream and Existence." It is our hope that the publication of this work, which has long been out of print and virtually unobtainable even in France, will help to shed new light on the formative years of Foucault's thought. It also serves as the occasion for focusing once more on Binswanger's pathbreaking analyses.

In bringing this special publication to fruition, the *Review* acknowledges its gratitude to many people. First, we would like to thank Michel Foucault himself for graciously granting permission for us to publish this English translation of his work, and allowing us to make this period of his work available to the English-speaking public. Second, we extend our thanks to Margot Backas and the Publications Program of the National Endowment for the Humanities for assistance in the form of a grant to aid in publication of this special issue. We also thank Jacob Needleman for kindly allowing us to print his translation of Binswanger's essay. And we heartily thank Forrest Williams for rendering Foucault's difficult French into excellent English, and providing an illuminating Preface as well.

NOTES

1 Michel Foucault, *Death and the Labyrinth: The World of Raymond Roussel*, trans. Charles Ruas (Garden City: Doubleday & Co., 1986), p. 174.

2 Martin Heidegger, *Being and Time*, trans. John Macquarrie and Edward Robinson (New York: Harper & Row, 1962).

3 Ludwig Binswanger, "Dream and Existence," trans. Jacob Needleman, *Review of Existential Psychology & Psychiatry*, Vol. XIX, no. 1 (1984-85). Also in *Being-in-the-World: Selected Papers of Ludwig Binswanger*, ed. and trans. Jacob Needleman (London: Souvenir Press, 1975).

4 Foucault, *Madness and Civilization: A History of Insanity in the Age of Reason*, trans. Richard Howard (New York: Random House, 1965).

5 Thomas Szasz, *The Myth of Mental Illness: Foundations of a Theory of Personal Conduct* (New York: Harper & Row, 1961).

6 R. D. Laing, *Self and Others* (New York: Random House, 1961).

7 David Cooper, "Introduction" to *Madness and Civilization* (London: Tavistock, 1961), p. viii.

8 Foucault, *Madness and Civilization*, pp. ix-xi.

9 Foucault, "Two Lectures," in *Power/Knowledge: Selected Interviews and Other Writings 1972-77*, ed. Colin Gordon (New York: Random House, 1980), p. 83.

10 Foucault, "Truth and Power," in *Power/Knowledge*, p. 109.

11 *See also* Hubert L. Dreyfus and Paul Rabinow, *Michel Foucault: Beyond Structuralism and Hermeneutics* (Chicago: University of Chicago Press, 1982), pp. xvii-xxvii.

12 Alan Sheridan, *Michel Foucault: The Will to Truth* (New York: Tavistock, 1980).

13 Dreyfus and Rabinow, *Michel Foucault*.

14 Foucault, "Dream, Imagination, and Existence," trans. Forrest Williams, *Review of Existential Psychology & Psychiatry*, Vol. XIX, no. 1 (1984-85); *Mental Illness and Psychology*, trans. Alan Sheridan (New York: Harper & Row, 1976; reprinted by University of California Press, 1987, forthcoming).

15 Foucault, *Mental Illness and Psychology*, p. 46.

16 Szasz, *The Myth of Mental Illness*.

17 Foucault, *Mental Illness and Psychology*, pp. 60 and 63.

18 *Ibid.*, pp. 78-79 and 86.

19 *Ibid.*, pp. 84-85.

20 Foucault, *Death and the Labyrinth*, p. 174.

21 *Ibid.*, pp. 174-75.

22 Foucault, *Power/Knowledge*, p. 117.

23 Edmund Husserl, *Phenomenological Psychology*, trans. John Scanlon (The Hague: Martinus Nijhoff, 1977), pp. 178-79.

24 *Ibid.*, p. 170.

25 Paul de Man, *Blindness and Insight* (Minneapolis: University of Minnesota Press, 1983²), p. 48.

26 *Ibid.*, pp. 48 and 49.

27 *Ibid.*, p. 49; Foucault, *The Order of Things* (New York: Random House, 1970), pp. 325-26. The translation cited is by de Man.

28 *Ibid.*, p. 49.

29 *Ibid.*

30 Herbert Spiegelberg, *Phenomenology in Psychology and Psychiatry* (Evanston: Northwestern University Press, 1972), p. 204.

31 Søren Kierkegaard, *Concluding Unscientific Postscript*, trans. David F. Swenson and Walter Lowrie (Princeton: Princeton University Press, 1941), p. 177. *See also* Spiegelberg, *Phenomenology in Psychology and Psychiatry*, p. 194. I am indebted to Professor Spiegelberg for locating the source of this quotation.

32 Kierkegaard, *Ibid.*, p. 176 and 177.

33 *Ibid.*, p. 223.

34 *Ibid.*, p. 183.

35 *Ibid.*, p. 177.

36 Binswanger, "Dream and Existence," *Review of Existential Psychology & Psychiatry*, Vol. XIX, no. 1 (1984-85).

37 *Ibid.*

38 *Ibid.*

39 *Ibid.*

Translator's Preface

FORREST WILLIAMS

The title "Dream, Imagination and Existence" has been added, but not arbitrarily, to this translation of the late Michel Foucault's "*Introduction*," published in 1954, to Ludwig Binswanger's essay, "Dream and Existence" (*Traum und Existenz; Le rêve et l'existence*). The nature of the essay as a whole, as well as the added title, were to have been subjects of discussion with Michel Foucault in Paris in July, 1984, at which time, as he had graciously expressed it in a letter a few months earlier, we were to "*continuer cette conversation*" begun the previous year during a visit to the University of Colorado. His sudden death on June 25, 1984, when he was only fifty-seven, occurred in a particularly prolific period of a brilliant intellectual career. His works were (and are) in bookstores everywhere in France and abroad. His newest writings were being translated as quickly as possible in a number of languages, generating the highest expectations for the remaining portions of his large-scale *History of Sexuality*.

The title assigned here attempts to specify the main themes of this early essay. And essay by Michel Foucault, not simply introduction to Ludwig Binswanger, it was. Almost twice the length of the work in clinical psychology it preceded, it stood as an independent piece of thought. Indeed, it specifically disclaimed being a mere explication (*ad usum delphinum*, as Foucault put it) of "Dream and Existence."

One of two pieces by the 28-year-old French thinker to appear in 1954, it was most likely the earlier of the pair, preceding his first book, *Mental Illness and Psychology* (New York: Harper and Row, 1976; *Maladie Mentale et Psychologie*, 1954), and therefore was probably his first extended piece of writing to be published. For so young an author, Foucault had already engaged in an imposing amount of philosophical study: figuring in the discussion are Edmund Husserl, Sigmund Freud, Martin Heidegger, Gaston Bachelard, Jean-Paul Sartre, and of course Ludwig Binswanger, as well as a variety of observations about dreams expressed in literature, drama, religion, and philosophies of other times. In the process of "introducing" the reader to Binswanger's Heideggerean transformation of Freudian psychoanalysis, Foucault went beyond the particular clinical concepts of Binswanger toward a more general analysis of human being, that is, of human being-in-the-world, without thereby (he insisted) "slipping into a philosophy." He did not wish either to restate Binswanger's psychology or to restate the philosophy of *Being and Time (Sein und Zeit)* presupposed by both Binswanger and himself. Neither psychotherapeutic theory nor transcendental phenomenology, Foucault's effort might be thought of as an intermediate essay in the direction of "existential anthropology," more specific than Heidegger's question of Being (*Seinsfrage*), more general then Binswanger's clinical reflections.

The identifying term of the German tradition of thought to which Foucault's essay belongs is, as is well known, the conspicuously ungermanic locution, *"Existenz."* Unfortunately, the word does not translate at all well into English (or into the romance languages). "Existence" and its cognates appear so frequently in our speech and writing that they lack the surprising air of *"Existenz"* when it appears in German texts. As we know, almost anything may be associated with the English word "existence": horses, centaurs, a cure for cancer, life on Mars, electrons, prime numbers, cabbages, bald French kings, and so on, *ad infinitum. "Existenz,"* by contrast, was introduced and consciously employed by certain German thinkers in part because of its comparative rarity in their language. (For example, Goethe put the word *"existieren"* in the mouth of Mephistopheles for its esoteric sound.) Thus, in the German writings of *Existenzphilosophie*, the term *"Existenz"* stands out, and serves to call explicit attention *solely* to the sort of being peculiar to the human being. In Foucault's text, therefore, the meaning is the Heideggerean one of the being of human being as transcendence toward the world. Such being is in contrast not only to the being of things, numbers, etc., but to the self-enclosed subject, characteristic of modern epistemology, which inwardly represents to itself a real world to which it is only externally related. In this translation, therefore, the alien term "Existenz" is used on occasion as a reminder of the special meaning of "existence" in the text.

Presuming, then, that his reader was already acquainted with the ontological notion of *Existenz* as a specific way of existing which transcends toward, or discloses, the world, and prompted by Binswanger's essay, "Dream and Existence," Foucault undertook what, as he declared at the outset, could only seem like an intellectual gamble: to seek fundamental features of human existence (*Existenz*), not in perception, but in the dream. For what, indeed, could seem *less* enlightening concerning existence, if it be a transcendence toward and presence to the world, than the apparent privacy, obscurity, and delusion of dreams? Psychologists, writers, and artists, particularly since Freud had interpreted dreams as symptoms or effects of unconscious intentions, have been fascinated by this strange phenomenon. And many philosophers, to be sure, have been intellectually fascinated by Freud's ideas. But the dream *itself*, as a phenomenon, has hardly been taken seriously in its own right in modern philosophy. On the contrary, philosophers have largely neglected their dreams. The celebrated discussion of dreaming by Descartes at the beginning of modern philosophy illustrates concisely this customary dismissal of the phenomenon of the dream. The 17th-century philosopher's aim was to advance his prior program of developing a theory of rational evidence and to supply a correct evaluation of the role of perception in the new science and in waking life. Descartes' attitude has been the standard one: the proper place of the dream in serious philosophical thought is as a foil for epistemological inquiry into the nature of perception.

There have been major philosophical exceptions, of course, of which Nietzsche, the most important single influence on Foucault's intellectual career, was an outstanding example. Still, for the most part, the received philosophical view has been that dreams are merely the tatters of integral human experience, with no evidential value in and of themselves, and with little enough to offer directly to the clarification of epistemological or ontological questions. Whereas waking experiences, and even waking illusions, are cherished as valuable resources for philosophical examination, the dream shrinks to a near-zero-point of human experience, far less useful to epistemology than the moral deficiency of a Nero has been to moral philosophy. In our times, dreams do not even need to be explicitly dismissed by philosophers, since they now may simply be abandoned to the discipline of psychoanalysis, where they may become intellectually interesting as symptoms or signs of something that happened in the past.

This philosophical neglect is understandable enough, no doubt. As we have already seen, Foucault openly acknowledged the difficulty, for a theory of existence (*Existenz*), of seeking in the dream, that seemingly most enclosed and cryptic of experiences, clarification of the ontological dimensions of human beings understood as transcendences toward the world. In his words: why turn to "a mode in which (human existence) is least engaged in the world," in which "the network of meanings seems to condense, where the evidence clouds over, and where the forms of presence to the world are most blurred?"

Yet one could adduce some reasons, even within the major epistemological program of modern philosophy, for taking dreams seriously. Modern theory of knowledge has not been preoccupied solely with perception and reason, but almost as much with imagination. In Kant's Critical philosophy, the schematism of the imagination may well be the fundamental epistemic function in human experience. If Foucault was right in his discussion, the customary neglect of the dream may well have invalidated our understanding of the nature of the imagination. For Foucault reversed the usual thesis that the dream is merely one variety of imagination and—on the usual account—a particularly aberrant form at that. Instead he proposed the uncommon thesis that "The dream is not a modality of the imagination, the dream is the first condition of its possibility." Thus, an adequate theory of the imagination—and hence, an adequate epistemology—presupposed for Foucault nothing less than an adequate grasp of the phenomenon of the dream. Far from the dream being a variation on the imagination, imagining is rooted in the dream. And more: the very character of existence is to be discerned in the oneiric. Yet this is not, he tried to show, a mere restatement of the importance of dreams asserted by Freud, for it involves a far more complex conception of meaning than can be found in psychoanalytic theory.

In effect, Foucault was carrying back to *"Träumlichkeit,"* to oneiric experience, Heidegger's *Daseinsanalytik* of everyday experience, of *"Alltäglichkeit."* Just as there was for Heidegger a levelled-out structure of "Anyone" (*das Man*) which provides important clues to the transcendental structure of *Dasein,* so Foucault, following Binswanger's psychoanalytic investigations, reflects on the dream as itself a kind of proto-intending of the world. A peculiarly intended world, certainly, but nevertheless not a mere absence of worldhood, not a mere "rhapsody of images" and associations. Thus, for Foucault, the notion of a "dream world" is to be taken quite seriously. Animated by an intentional structure, it aims, as does perceptual experience, at a meaningful whole—even if a mutilated, truncated one, even if self-transcendence toward worldhood is here a "false start," as it were. Modern epistemology has not been wrong, therefore, to think of the dream as a kind of failed perception; but it has not been right, either, in measuring the human significance of the dream exclusively as a general failure of something else, as non-perception, as lack. The quasi-world of the dream is an already specific, and hence ontologically instructive failure, much as zoological sports are instructive. Save that the dream is not an oddity, but a regular feature of our existence. It is a quasi-world, containing neglected information about ourselves, not only for clinical psychologists interested in deciphering our individual neuroses and psychoses, but for our reflective understanding of the originative movement or project by which we transcend ourselves as *Dasein* or beings-in-the-world. Thus, the dream served Foucault in this essay somewhat as the brain-injured "Schneider" served Merleau-Ponty in the *Phenomenology of Perception* (a work by which Foucault was much influenced at that time). Sometimes, as we know, the discarded sketches of an artist are most revealing precisely because of the evident frustration of their generative aims.

The dream world for Foucault was that paradox (in the Heraclitean phrase he cited several times) of an *idios kosmos,* a "world of its own." As *idios,* it is solely mine, unlike the world *tout court,* which is *ours.* Yet as *kosmos,* the dream is not a merely subjective phenomenon: it already has the lineaments, the prefigurations, of transcendence and worldhood. It is not pure immanence. Foucault thus directs upon the phenomenon of dreams the same kind of assault on the subject-object dichotomy that had been mounted on perception by Heidegger and Merleau-Ponty on the basis of their readings of Husserl's radical undermining of the representational theory of perception. If to perceive things is not to represent them more or less veridically in some inner place, then to dream cannot be a merely degraded and uninformative version of such representations. To perceive is itself a way of being-in-the-world, and to dream is already on the way to such being-in-the-world. In the order of inquiry, the dream, not the perception, comes first. Case histories of clinical psychology at once become interesting, not for their pathology alone (however important that may be), but for their wider revelation of the pre-perceptual structure of human intentionality and presence to the world. Foucault's essay thus boldly undercuts the basis of *Being and Time* and *Phenomenology of Perception*. Already the dream "in and by its transcendence...discloses the original movement by which existence, in its irreducible solitude, projects itself toward a world which constitutes itself as the setting of its history." The dynamic vectors of existence are already discernible in the dream.

And likewise, the inherent temporality of human existence. Indeed, one might say that Freudian dream analysis, by concentrating on earlier, repressed wishes said to be causing dreams, denied the temporality of the patient as existence. Literary, philosophical, and mystical accounts, even superstitious beliefs, frequently recognized that the dream is at once an effect of the past (for example, some past deed), an occurrence in the present, and an anticipation (e.g., an omen) of the future. Mythological views and prophecies aside, there was at least in those traditional concep- tions of the dream an acknowledgment of its temporality and—by impli- cation—of the temporality of the being of the dreamer.

As an example of the Freudian neglect of the future orientation of the dream (which is to say, its Freudian detemporalization), Foucault points to a dream of "Dora," in which Freud had failed to recognize soon enough the patient's decision, still unknown to herself, to terminate the psychoanalysis.

One might formulate the issue as follows: Because the classic scien- tific spirit which animated Freud's thinking characteristically separates past, present, and future, the psychoanalytic patient's existence is rendered only abstractly temporal, like an object in the natural sciences. Standing only in external relations to each other, as mere logical distinctions in a formal pattern of succession which is abstracted from the concrete phenomenon of becoming, the so-called "pasts," "presents," and "futures" of the natural sciences are virtually timeless. This is an entirely appropriate philosophical (in Heideggerean terms: still ontic) framework for the par- ticular theoretical purposes of the algorithmic sciences. Only in this time- less framework does it make sense to speak of causal *laws*—ideally, equations with empirical constants. But once conceived in this manner, as separable, these Pickwickian "pasts," "presents," and "futures" fragment the phenomenon of time. The so-called "future," for example, is no longer what is approaching the present, and the present is no longer falling back into a past. The "future" is already in place, though not yet visible to us, like the furniture in an adjoining room which we have not yet entered. Thus, the "grammar" of that "future" which a causal law predicts (more or less successfully) contains no future tense as such, but only the future perfect. The "present" event whose "past" causes can be stated, or the "future" event which can be predicted—it makes no difference whether one moves backward or forward from the given, since time is incidental— is, relative to the so called "past," not an event which is itself genuinely passing. Strictly speaking, from the standpoint of causal explanation, all events are in truth events which *shall have been*. Causal theory does exploit temporal *distinctions*, obviously, but only after *first* divesting them of their temporality. The objects of the natural sciences are thus *a*temporal constructs, and so are Freud's psychoanalytic cases, for all the emphasis— indeed, precisely because of the psychoanalytic emphasis—on the patient's past. In human existence (*Existenz*), however—and here Foucault followed Heidegger to the letter—temporality is our inescapable way of being, and therefore requires another way of speaking about human beings and about their dreams. To understand the dream as an (incipient) way of being-in- the-world is the only way to respect the temporality of the being of the dreamer and thus to approach and analyze the dream in its necessarily temporal integrity: in (to use Heidegger's language) its threefold "ecstatic" character. To be-in-the-world, to exist, and to be temporal, are inseparable ontological features of *Dasein*. The logical construct of "time" which is indispensable to the natural sciences, and to which Freudian theory appears to subscribe, fits human beings only to the degree that they may be appropriately viewed as objects. In some respects and for some purposes, they definitely may be. But certainly not as dreamers.

If Foucault was right, then, the quasi-world of the dream is not just some effect that results from an earlier time, nor some particular event that just happens during sleep, like indigestion or sexual arousal, any more than being present to the world in perception is some particular, contingent event within our waking life, like stumbling on a rock or misunderstanding a question. Like the perceptual world with its instru- mental agencies, invitations to knowledge, and social intercourse, the dream, with its bizarre images, is a quasi-world, a fundamental mode of our being-in-the-world, and hence an "experience" with its own kind of elusive totality and meaningful structure. Its significance and its structure cannot be understood by reference only to the past, especially to a past which is externally related to the dream.

The Freudian will reply, of course, that unconscious intentions, the "latent meanings" of the dream, are precisely what render the connection with the earlier events more than merely external. The Freudian conception of language and meaning, however, proves on Foucault's analysis to be no less defective than its conception of temporality. In a fascinating jux- taposition of two great thinkers, Foucault brought together his study of Husserl's *Logical Investigations* and Freud's *Interpretation of Dreams*. A delicious irony emerging from his comparison of these two celebrated works is his demonstration that Freud the empirical scientist took far too abstract a view of meaning, and Husserl the logician provided the far more concrete analysis. Foucault had already discerned in 1954 what is still largely unacknowledged by those Husserlians of the 70's and 80's who continue to try to assimilate Husserl's theory of meaning to that of Frege. Foucault correctly perceived that Husserl was concerned, from the very beginning, not with "sense" and "reference" alone (Frege's *Sinn* and *Bedeutung*), as these attach formally to combinations of words or concepts, but with *the full intentional phenomenon of expression (Ausdruck)*: the question of how meaning *animates* the symbol. The "Fregean-Husserlian" scholars properly point out that Husserl's "noema" was "a generalization of the notion of linguistic meaning." However, they tend to ignore what Husserl understood by "linguistic meaning," which is not adequately represented within the Fregean conception of language they often attribute to Husserl. For Husserl, to mean is *always an expressive act*. It is therefore essential for the reader to recognize that the Husserl evoked by Foucault in 1954 to improve on Freud's conception of the dream as symbol was not the trimmed-down, formal logician currently popularized in contemporary analytic philosophy, and cut to resemble Frege, but the *phenomenologist of intentional expression*. (The latter is the Husserl evoked nowadays in the writings of J. N. Mohanty, Paul Ricoeur, Dallas Willard and others.) "The word," as Foucault wrote in his essay, "implies a world of expression which precedes it, sustains it."

Yet another criticism of Freudian theory to be found in Foucault's essay has to do with the "I" or subject of the dream. In opposition to Freud's identification of the dream "I" with a represented subject—either bearing the dreamer's own features or, by displacement, bearing another's features—Foucault proposed that the whole dream, and everything in it, may be regarded as its true "I." This "pan-egoic" view, as it might be called, echoed a fundamental change in therapeutic dream-analysis which had in fact been initiated independently and at about the same time by the Freudian dissenter from psychoanalytic orthodoxy, Frederick S. Perls, whose revisions of dream theory had originated in studies of Gestalt psychology. The general implications of this conceptual modification are only briefly illustrated in Foucault's essay; the detailed implications, for both dream analysis and for practical techniques of psychotherapy, were yet to be worked out, in the 50's and 60's, by the late Dr. Perls.

Foucault was also able to propose in his essay a criticism of Sartre's theory of the imagination, which he regarded as still too dependent upon a negative definition that contrasted imagination with perception. Thus, the very accusation that had already been leveled by Sartre against earlier theories of the image from classical Greece to Bergson, is charged against Sartre as well. For Foucault, as we have noted, saw the dream, not as a degenerated variety of imagining, a kind of "rhapsody" of the life of images, but as the parent of the imagination. This reversal, this appropriation of imagining to dreaming, led Foucault to a surprising account of poetic imagery as the gelling of poetic expression, and thus to a conception of the poetically expressed as transcending the images with which it is usually identified. In poetic expression, images negotiate transcendence, but also neutralize each other. The expressive reality of the poem is thus trans-imaginal. The influence of Gaston Bachelard's remarkable writings on the key images of earth, air, fire and water is acknowledged by Foucault, but he was already probing beyond Bachelard's view, as he had gone beyond Sartre's view, in his reflections on imagination and poetry.

Finally, in the way of critique, there emerges already in this first, phenomenologically-oriented essay, with its superb phenomenological analyses (*viz.*, Foucault's vivid variation on Sartre's "absent Peter"), a certain dissatisfaction with phenomenology. Foucault saw phenomenology as indispensable for recapturing the expressive character of intentionality, for characterizing temporality and its three "ecstasies," for carrying through a Binswangerian reform of Freudian psychoanalytic theory, and most of all, for understanding the existential significance of dreams and images; but he also saw it as insufficient to capture the reality of others—the challenge, of course, with which Husserl wrestled in the *Cartesian Meditations* and elsewhere. In view of these reservations in the earliest of his writings, it is not surprising that we do not find Foucault calling himself a "phenomenologist" in his subsequent writings, despite his debt to that tradition of modern philosophy. One might even wonder, looking at the most recently published works of Michel Foucault, whether they could have been written by the author of the essay published here. Nevertheless, there are anticipations—which is not to say, pre-determinations—in the early essay of some themes of the subsequent thirty years of work. For example, Foucault's critique in his 1954 essay of certain classical primacies and oppositions (subject and object, perception and dream) were based on a belief that there is something philosophically instructive about the very persistence of these historic polarities. He was already suspicious, it seems, of the usual primacy assigned to the "normal" case (e.g., perception, or even imagination) over the "abnormal" case (e.g., dreaming). Is it too much to say that in his insistence upon their interrelation, and in this scepticism regarding the "norm," were prefigured his later interest in a variety of such polarities in modern discourse. Did he not detect in the usual treatment of the dream a kind of scapegoating of a mode of human experience, a scapegoating which was to be exposed again and again as he studied the history of systems of discourse and the strategies of power? Were not his later analyses of the intimate, diacritical relation between "reason" and "madness" of the modern classical age perhaps suggested by his quasi-rehabilitation in 1954 of the dream from the benign neglect to which modern epistemology had consigned it? (Cf. *Madness and Civilization*, New York: Pantheon, 1965; *Histoire de la folie*, 1961.)

Certainly, we must emphasize that the later Foucault moved away from his early epistemological, phenomenological, and transcendental stance to a different mode of inquiry which he named "archaeology." Then, finding that conception still too much in the transcendental or justificational spirit of the Enlightenment, he moved to an even more historically conscious "genealogy." His later works were thus increasingly indebted to Nietzsche, who had already been brought vividly to the young Foucault's attention (shortly after the war by the French philosopher Jean Wahl, whose boundless curiosity and energetic teaching brought so many new currents of thought, from both the 19th and 20th centuries, into the lecture halls of the Sorbonne and into French intellectual life.) Later, of course, Nietzsche became the pre-eminent influence on Foucault's thought. Perhaps it is even fair to say, on the evidence of this 1954 essay, that Foucault was from the beginning already a philosopher of language and of desire, and possibly (from remarks here and there), a philosopher of social history.

However, the early concern with linguistic meaning as act of expression later expanded, far beyond anything visible in 1954, to linguistic complexes of discourse which function as historically active, social strategies of power inscribed in our very bodies. The empirical bent revealed in his early preoccupation with the case histories of Freud and Binswanger found new scope in his later studies of the actual institutions of prison, madhouse, hospital, courtroom, medical profession; historical studies which served to subtend his inquiries into the linguistic structures of power condensed in such received oppositions as "the sane and the mad," "the *bon citoyen* and the criminal," "the normal and the pathological." None of these now much-discussed writings, nor the apparently unfinished "magnum opus, *Histoire de la Sexualité*, could have been foreseen in this essay of over thirty years ago. Yet, whatever its late author might have wished to say of this early work in July, 1984—which, sadly, was not to be said—this essay does appear to contain a few of the elements of his later writings; and, more important, seems to stand in its own right as one of the few genuinely thoughtful investigations in our times of the relations between dreaming, imagining, and *Existenz*.

NOTES ON THE TRANSLATION

The work by Michel Foucault translated here from the French appeared originally as an "Introduction" to the French translation (by Jacqueline Verdeaux) of Ludwig Binswanger's *Traum und Existenz*. The latter work was originally published in *Neue Schweizer Rundshau* (Zürich: Fretz u. Wasmuth), v. IX, 1930, and was reprinted in Ludwig Binswanger, *Ausgewählte Vorträge und Aufsätze* (Bern; A. Francke, 1947, pp. 74-97). The French volume was entitled *Le rêve et l'existence*, and was published in Paris in 1954 by Éditions Desclée De Brouwer in the series *Textes et Études Anthropologiques*. The "Introduction" comprised pages 9-128; the text by Binswanger comprised pages 129-193.

*

The "Translator's Preface" contains some remarks on the occasional use of the special German term, "*Existenz*," in the English translation.

*

Translations of passages quoted by Foucault from the works of the French poet, René Char, were most kindly supplied by Mary Ann Caws.

*

Wherever possible, fragmentary footnotes have been completed for the English translation, and references have been adapted to English-language sources where these exist and were discoverable. French paragraphing has been modified to conform to American editorial practice, and some subdividing has been added.

*

I would like to express my appreciation for released time to work on this preface and translation provided by the Center for Theory in the Humanities of the University of Colorado at Boulder.

DREAM, IMAGINATION AND EXISTENCE

Michel Foucault

À l'âge d'homme, j'ai vu s'élever et grandir sur le mur mitoyen de la vie et de la mort, une échelle de plus en plus nue, investie d'un pouvoir d'evulsion unique: le rêve . . . Voici que l'obscurité s'écarte, et que VIVRE devient sous la forme d'un âpre ascétisme allégorique la conquête des pouvoirs extraordinaires dont nous nous sentons confusément traversés mais que nous n'exprimons qu'incomplètement faute de loyauté, de discernement cruel et de persévérance.

When I reached manhood, I saw rising and growing upon the wall shared between life and death, a ladder barer all the time, invested with an unique power of evulsion: this was the dream...Now see darkness draw away, and LIVING become, in the form of a harsh allegorical asceticism, the conquest of extraordinary powers by which we feel ourselves confusedly crossed, but which we only express incompletely, lacking loyalty, cruel perception, and perseverence.

René Char, *Fureur et Mystère* (Paris: Gallimard, 1984, 2nd ed.), pp. 82-83 ("Partage Formel, XXII"). Translated by Mary Ann Caws.

Dream, Imagination and Existence*

An Introduction to Ludwig Binswanger's "Dream and Existence"

MICHEL FOUCAULT

Translated by Forrest Williams

I

In these introductory pages we do not intend to retrace, according to the familiar paradox of prefaces, the path taken by Ludwig Binswanger himself in "Dream and Existence" (*Traum und Existenz*). The difficulty of this text suggests doing so, no doubt. But its difficulty is too essential to its line of reflection to be attenuated in a zealous foreword *ad usum delphini*, even if the "psychologist" remains always the dauphin in the kingdom of reflection. Original forms of thought are their own introduction: their history is the only kind of exegesis that they permit, and their destiny, the only kind of critique.

Yet it is not its history either which we shall attempt to decipher here. In another work we shall try to situate existential analysis within the development of contemporary reflection on man, and try to show, by observing the inflection of phenomenology toward anthropology, what foundations have been proposed for concrete reflection on man. Here, these introductory remarks have only one purpose: to present a form of analysis which does not aim at being a philosophy, and whose end is not to be a psychology; a form of analysis which is fundamental in relation to all concrete, objective, and experimental knowledge; a form of analysis, finally, whose principle and method are determined from the start solely by the absolute privilege of their object: man, or rather, the being of man, *Menschsein*.

The working dimensions of anthropology can thereby be circumscribed.[1] It is an undertaking which opposes anthropology to any type of psychological positivism claiming to exhaust the significant content of man by the reductive concept of *homo natura*. It relocates anthropology within the context of an ontological reflection whose major theme is presence-to-being, existence (*Existenz*), *Dasein*.[2] Granted, an anthropology of this sort can validate itself only by showing how an analysis of human being can be articulated upon an analytic of existence. As a problematic of foundations, it must define in the latter the conditions of

*This "Introduction" originally appeared in *Le rêve et l'existence*, by Ludwig Binswanger (Paris: Desclée de Brouwer, 1954), pp. 8-128. The *Review* is extremely grateful to Michel Foucault for kindly granting permission to publish this first English translation. According to his recollection, it was written in 1953 while he was a doctoral student in Paris. (KH, *Ed.*)

possibility of the former. As a problem of justification, it must set out the appropriate dimensions and the autochthonous meaning of anthropology.

Let us say provisionally (pending some later revisions) that human being (*Menschsein*) is nothing but the actual and concrete content which ontology analyzes as the transcendental structure of *Dasein*, of presence-to-the-world. Thus, this basic opposition to any science of human facts of the order of positive knowledge, experimental analysis, and naturalistic reflection does not refer anthropology to some a priori form of philosophical speculation. The theme of inquiry is the human "fact," if one understands by "fact," not some objective sector of a natural universe, but the real content of an existence which is living itself and is experiencing itself, which recognizes itself or loses itself, in a world that is at once the plenitude of its own project and the "element" of its situation. Anthropology may thus call itself a "science of facts" by developing in rigorous fashion the existential content of presence-to-the-world. To reject such an inquiry at first glance because it is neither philosophy nor psychology, because one cannot define it as either science or speculation, because it neither looks like positive knowledge nor provides the content of a priori cognition, is to ignore the basic meaning of the project.[3]

It has seemed to us worthwhile to follow *for a moment* this path of reflection, and to see whether the reality of man may not prove to be accessible only outside any distinction between the psychological and the philosophical; whether man, in his forms of existence, may not be the only means of getting to man.

In contemporary anthropology, the approach of Binswanger seems to us to take the royal road. He outflanks the problem of ontology and anthropology by going straight to concrete existence, to its development and its historical content. Thence, by way of an analysis of the structures of existence (*Existenz*)—of this very existence which bears such and such a name and has traversed such and such a history—he moves continually back and forth between the anthropological forms and the ontological conditions of existence. He continually crosses a dividing line that seems so difficult to draw, or rather, he sees it ceaselessly crossed by a concrete existence in which the real limit of *Menschsein* and *Dasein* is manifested. Hence, nothing could be more mistaken than to see in Binswanger's analyses an "application" of the concept and methods of the philosophy of existence to the "data" of clinical experience. It is a matter, for him, of bringing to light, by returning to the concrete individual, the place where the forms and conditions of existence articulate. Just as anthropology resists any attempt to divide it into philosophy and psychology, so the existential analysis of Binswanger avoids any a priori distinction between ontology and anthropology. One avoids the distinction without eliminating it or rendering it impossible: it is relocated at the terminus of an inquiry whose point of departure is characterized not by a line of division, but by an encounter with concrete existence.

To be sure, this encounter, and no less surely, the status that is finally to be assigned to the ontological conditions, pose problems. *But we leave that issue to another time.* We only want to show that one can enter straightway into the analyses of Binswanger and get to what they signify by an approach no less primordial, no less basic, than that by which he himself reaches the concrete existence of his patients. Detouring through a more or less Heideggerean philosophy is not some initiatory rite which might open a door to the esotericism of the analysis of Dasein. The philosophical problems are there; but they are not preconditions.

Therefore, we may dispense with an introduction which summarizes *Being and Time* (*Sein und Zeit*) in numbered paragraphs, and we are free to proceed less rigorously. Our proposal is only to write in the margins of "Dream and Existence."

*

The theme of this 1930 essay[4]—the first of the texts of Binswanger which belong strictly to the analysis of Dasein[5]—is less dream *and* existence than existence as it appears to itself and can be deciphered in the dream: existence in that mode of being of the dream in which it announces itself in a meaningful fashion. Is it not a gamble, however, to want to circumscribe the positive content of *Existenz* by reference to a mode in which it is least engaged in the world? If *Menschsein* does contain meanings which are peculiar to it, will they reveal themselves in a privileged way in that dream moment when the network of meanings seems to condense, where the evidence clouds over, and where the forms of presence are most blurred?

This paradox constitutes, in our opinion, the major interest of "Dream and Existence." The privilege of meaning accorded by Binswanger to the oneiric is doubly important. It defines the concrete progression of the analysis toward the fundamental forms of existence: dream analysis does not stop at the level of a hermeneutic of symbols. Rather, starting from an external interpretation which is still only a kind of deciphering, it is able, without slipping into a philosophy, to arrive at a comprehension of existential structures. The meaning of the dream continually deploys itself from the cipher of the appearance to the modalities of existence. On the other hand, this privileged status of dream experience silently encompasses, in this text, a whole anthropology of the imagination that requires a new definition of the relations between meaning and symbol, between image and expression—in short, a new way of conceiving how meanings are manifested.

These two aspects of the problem will occupy us in the ensuing pages. All the more so to the degree that Binswanger has left them unclarified. We are not trying to parcel out credit to be sure, but rather trying to express in this way what it is to "recognize" a line of thought that brings us even more than it says, while still hoping to remain properly modest toward its history.

II

A coincidence of dates is worth underscoring: 1899, Husserl's *Logical Investigations*; 1900, Freud's *Interpretation of Dreams*. Twofold attempt by man to recapture his meanings and to recapture himself in his significance.

With the *Interpretation of Dreams*, the dream makes its entry into the field of human meanings. In the dream experience the meaning of behavior seems to blur. As waking consciousness darkens and flickers out, the dream seems to loosen, and finally to untie, the knot of meanings. Dream had been taken as if it were the nonsense of consciousness. We know how Freud turned this proposition around, making the dream the meaning of the unconscious. This shift from the meaninglessness of the dream to the disclosure of its hidden meaning, and the whole hermeneutic labor involved, have frequently been emphasized. Much importance has also been assigned to the reification of the unconscious, as psychic authority and latent content. Much, and even too much: to the point of neglecting another aspect of the problem which, insofar as it puts into question the relations of meaning and image, is our concern here.

The imaginary forms of the dream carry the implicit meanings of the unconscious; in the penumbra of dream life, they lend these meanings a quasi-presence. Yet, precisely the presence of meaning in the dream is not meaning making itself fully evident. The dream betrays the meaning even as it effects it, offering it only while ephemeralizing it. The fire that means sexual fire—shall we say that it is there only to point to that meaning, or to attenuate the meaning, to hide it and obscure it by a new glow? There are two ways to answer this question.

One way is along functional lines. The meaning is assigned as much "counter-meaning" as necessary to cover the whole surface of the dream realm. The dream is the fulfillment of a desire, but if it is dream and not fulfilled desire, that is precisely because the dream also answers to all the "counter desires" which oppose the desire itself. The dream fire is the burning satisfaction of sexual desire, but what makes the desire take shape in the subtle substance of fire is everything that denies this desire and ceaselessly tries to extinguish it. The dream is a functional composite, and if the meaning is invested in images, this is by way of a surplus, a multiplication of meanings which override and contradict each other. The imaginative plasticity of the dream is, for the meaning which comes to light in it, but the form of its contradictoriness.

Nothing more. The image is exhausted in the multiplicity of meanings. Its morphological structure, the space in which it deploys itself, its temporal rhythm of development, in short, the world which it bears with it, all these count for nothing if they are not allusions to these meanings. In other words, the language of the dream is analyzed only in its semantic function. Freudian analysis leaves its morphological and syntactic structure in the dark. The distance between meaning and image is closed, in the analytical interpretation, only by an excess of meaning; the image in its fullness is determined by over-determination. The peculiarly imaginative dimension of the meaningful expression is completely omitted.

And yet, it is not a matter of indifference that such and such an image embodies such and such a meaning—that sexuality be water or fire, that the father be a subterranean demon or a solar force. It is important that the image possesses its own dynamic powers, that there is a different morphology of space when it is free, luminous space and when the space put into play is imprisoning, dark, and stifling. The imaginary world has its own laws, its specific structures, and the image is somewhat more than the immediate fulfillment of meaning. It has its own density, and the laws which govern it are not solely significant propositions, just as the laws of the world are not simply decrees of will, even a divine will. Freud caused the world of the imaginary to be inhabited by Desire as classical metaphysics caused the world of physics to be inhabited by Divine Will and Understanding: a theology of meanings, in which the truth anticipates its own formulations and completely constitutes them. The meanings exhaust the reality of the world which displays that reality.

One might say that psychoanalysis gave the dream no status beyond that of speech, and failed to see it in its reality as language. But that was both risky and paradoxical: if the word seems to lose itself in the meaning that it wants to bring to light, if it seems to exist only by and for the signification, the word is nevertheless possible only by way of a language that exists in rigorous syntactic rules and in the solid impress of morphological shapes. The word, to say something, implies a world of expression which precedes it, sustains it, and allows it to give body to what it means. By failing to acknowledge this structure of language, which dream experience, like every expressive fact, necessarily envelops, Freudian psychoanalysis of dreams never gets a comprehensive grasp of meaning. Meaning does not appear, for psychoanalysis, through recognition of a linguistic structure, but must be extracted, deduced, gleaned from a word taken by itself. And dream interpretation, naturally, becomes a method designed to discover the meanings of words in a language whose grammar one does not understand: it becomes a method of cross-referencing of the sort used by the archaeologist for lost languages, a method of probabilistic confirmation, as in the deciphering of secret codes, a method of meaningful coincidings as in the most traditional arts of divination. The boldness of such methods and the risks do not invalidate their results. Nevertheless, the uncertainty of the starting point is never entirely dispelled by the constantly increasing probability that develops within the analysis itself, not entirely eliminated by the number of cases that come to sanction a kind of interindividual lexicon of the most frequent symbolizations. Freudian analysis retrieves only one meaning among the many possible meanings by the shortcut of divination or the longer route of probability. The expressive act itself is never reconstituted in its necessity.

Psychoanalysis gets only to the hypothetical, thus generating one of the most fundamental paradoxes of the Freudian conception of the image. Whenever analysis tries to exhaust the whole content of the image in the meaning it may secrete, the link uniting image to meaning is always defined as a possible, eventual, contingent one. Why does the psychological meaning take shape in an image, instead of remaining implicit or dissolving into the limpidity of a verbal formulation? By what means does the meaning insert itself within the malleable destiny of an image?

Freud gives a twofold answer to this question. As a result of repression, the meaning cannot acquire a clear formulation. In the density of the image, meaning finds the wherewithal to express itself allusively. The image is a language which expresses without formulating, an utterance less transparent for meaning than the word itself. And, on the other hand, Freud presupposes the primitively imaginative character of the satisfaction of desire. In the primitive consciousness, archaic or infantile, desire first finds satisfaction in the narcissistic and irreal mode of fantasy, and in the regression of the dream this original mode of fulfillment is revealed. One sees how Freud was led to rediscover in his theoretical mythology the themes that had been excluded in the hermeneutic stage of this interpretation of dreams.

He thus reinstates the notion of some necessary and original link between image and meaning, and admits that the structure of the image has a syntax and a morphology irreducible to the meaning; for the meaning, precisely, manages to hide itself in the expressive forms of the image. Yet, despite the presence of these two themes, because of the purely abstract form in which Freud leaves them, one looks in vain in his work for a grammar of the imaginary modality, and for an analysis of the expressive act in its necessity.

An inadequate elaboration of the notion of symbol is doubtless at the origin of these defects of Freudian theory. Freud takes the symbol as merely the tangential point where, for an instant, the limpid meaning joins with the material of the image taken as a transformed and transformable residue of perception. The symbol is that surface of contact, that film, which separates, as it joins, an inner world and an external world; the instantiation of an unconscious impulse and of a perceptual consciouness;

the factor of implicit language and the factor of sensible image.

Nowhere more than in his analysis of Senate President Schreber did Freud try to examine this place of contact. The privileged case of a crime exhibited in effect the constant presence of meaning at work in an imaginary world, and showed the structure belonging to this world through its reference to the meaning. But in the course of the analysis Freud finally abandoned this attempt, and located his reflections on two different levels. On one level, he established symbolic correlations which enable one to detect beneath the image of the solar god, the Father figure, and beneath the Ahriman image, the person of the patient himself. And on another level, he analyzed meanings, while this fantasy world remains no more than one possible expression of them. Reducing meanings to their most transparent verbal expression, he thus purifies them, proffering an extraordinary emotional declension, the magical framework of paranoid delirium: "I don't love him, I hate him," "It isn't he whom I love, it's she whom I love, because she loves me," "It isn't I who love the man, it's she who loves him"—declensions whose first form and simplest semantic character amount to: "I love her," and whose ultimate form, reached through all the contradictory inflections, emerges quite to the contrary as: "I don't love anyone at all, I love only myself."[6]

If the analysis of the Schreber case is so important in Freud's work, it is just to the extent that the distance has never been so shortened between a psychology of meaning transcribed into a psychology of language, and a psychology of the image expanded into a psychology of fantasy. At the same time, nowhere in psychoanalysis has the possibility of finding a connection between these two orders of analysis been more decisively precluded. Or, if you like, the impossibility of a serious treatment of a psychology of the Imago—to the extent that one can term "Imago" an imaginary structure taken in all its meaningful implications.

The history of psychoanalysis seems to bear out our contention, since to this day the gap has not been reduced. We see these two tendencies, which at one time were seeking each other out, moving further and further apart. There are analyses along the lines of Melanie Klein, which turn on the genesis, development, and crystallization of fantasies, recognized as in some way the primary material of the psychological experience. And there are analyses along the lines of Jacques Lacan, which seek in language the dialectical element where the ensemble of existential meanings are constituted and find their destiny, just insofar as the word, remaining outside all dialogue, fails to negotiate, through an *Aufhebung*, the deliverance and transmutation of the meanings. Melanie Klein has doubtless done the most to retrace the genesis of meaning from the movement of fantasy alone. Lacan for his part has done everything possible to show in the Imago the point at which the meaningful dialogue of language seizes up and becomes spellbound by the interlocutor it constituted. But for the former the meaning is basically nothing but the mobility of the image and the path, as it were, of its trajectory; and for the latter the Imago is but a muffled world, a moment of silence. In the realm of psychoanalytic investigation, therefore, the unity between a psychology of the image which demarcates the field of presence, and a psychology of meaning which defines the field of linguistic potentialities, has not been found.

Psychoanalysis has never succeeded in making images speak.

*

The *Logical Investigations* are curiously contemporaneous with the hermeneutic of the *Interpretation of Dreams*. Within the rigor of the analyses conducted the length of the First and Sixth of these investigations, can one find a theory of symbol and sign which reinstates in its necessity the immanence of the meaning to the image?

Psychoanalysis had taken the term "symbol" as immediately valid, without trying to develop or even to delimit it. By "symbolic value of the dream image" Freud really had two quite distinct things in mind. On the one hand, he had in mind the set of objective indices which betoken in the image implicit structures, earlier events, experiences that remained silent. Morphological similarities, dynamic analogies, syllabic identities and all sorts of word games, these constitute so many objective indices in the image, so many allusions to that which the image does not manifest in its colorful fullness.

On the other hand, there is the global and significant link which founds the meaning of the dream material and constitutes it as a dream of incestuous desire, of infantile regression, or of return and narcissistic envelopment. The set of indices can multiply indefinitely as the meaning progresses and unifies, and cannot therefore be confounded with the meaning. They arise along the path of inductive probabilities and are never more than the method of reconstituting the latent content or the original meaning. As for the meaning itself, it can only be brought to light in a comprehensive grasp, for it is by its own movement that it founds the symbolic value of the dream image. The confusing of these two things has inclined psychoanalysis to describe the mechanisms of the formation of dreams as the reverse and the correlative of the methods of reconstitution, confounding the achievement of meanings with the induction of indices.

In the first of the *Logical Investigations*, Husserl rightly distinguished between the index and the signification.[7] No doubt in phenomena of expression these are intermingled to the point that one tends to confound them. When someone speaks, we understand what he says not only by a meaningful grasp of the words he uses and the sentence structures he puts into play, but we also let ourselves be guided by the vocal melody, which now modulates and trembles, now assumes the hardness and glow by which we recognize anger. In this global comprehension these two attitudes, however mingled, are not identical. They are inverse and complementary, since it is above all when the words begin to elude me, distorted by distance, by noise, or by the stridency of the voice, that induction of indices becomes more prominent than comprehension of meaning: the tone of voice, the volume of words, the silences, even the verbal slips, will guide me and cause me to presume that my interlocutor is choking with rage.

By itself the index has no signification, and only in a secondary way can it acquire one, by the oblique route of a consciousness which uses it as a marker, a reference, or a token.

I see some holes in the snow, some regularly-shaped stars, some crystalline shadows. A hunter would see the fresh tracks of a hare. We have here two lived situations. It would be idle to say that one contains more truth than the other. However, the essence of indication is exhibited in the latter, not in the former. Only for the hunter is the little star *pressed down into* the snow, i.e., a sign. This does not mean that the hunter has more associative material than I do, that to his perception is associated an image of the hare which, in the same situation, I lacked. The associating is derivative in relation to the structure of indication. Association only goes over with full strokes the dotted lines of a structure already given in the essence of indicator and indicated. "Association recalls contents to consciousness while leaving it to them to attach themselves to given contents according to the law of their respective essences."[8]

But this essential structure, on which the psychological moment rests—on what does it, in turn, rest? On an actual situation that exists, or will exist, or has existed. The traces on the snow refer to the real hare who has just bounded away. The trembling voice is, according to its modulation, an index of exploding anger, or of mounting anger, or of anger which, with great difficulty, is containing and calming itself. Whereas the authentic sign, to be significant, does not need to rest on any objective situation: when I utter the word "hare," I may be referring to the one that raced the tortoise; when I mentioned my rage, I was speaking of a surge of passion which I have never experienced except in pretense or in a play. The words "hare" or "rage" are meaningful, the strident voice, the trace impressed in the snow, are indices.

A phenomenology of the dream, to be rigorous, must not fail to distinguish between indicative elements, which may designate for the analyst an objective situation they betoken, and significant contents which constitute, from within, the dream experience.

But what is a significant content, and what relation does it bear to an imaginary content? Here, too, certain analyses of the *Logical Investigations* can serve as a point of departure. It is not legitimate to allow, as psychoanalysis does, an immediate identity between meaning and image, united in the unique notion of symbol. The essence of the act of signification must be sought beyond, and even before, the verbal expression or the image structure in which it may be embodied.

> The acts of formulation, of imagination, of perception, are too diverse for signification to exhaust itself now in these, now in those. We must opt for a conception which attributes this function of signification to a single act which is everywhere identical, to an act which is free of the limits of a perception that may so often be lacking.[9]

What are the characteristics of this fundamental act? Negatively speaking, one sees at once that it cannot consist in relating one or more images. As Husserl notes, if we think of a chiliagon, we imagine, no matter what, a polygon with a lot of sides.[10] More positively, an act of signification, even the most thwarted, the most elementary, the most bound-up in some perceptual content, opens onto a new horizon. Even when I say this spot is red, or even in the exclamation, "This spot," even when I lack the words and I point my finger at something before me, an act of aiming is constituted that breaks with the immediate horizon of perception and discloses the signifying essence of the lived perception: the act of meaning this (*der Akt des Diesmeinens*).

This act is not definable (as our example suffices to demonstrate) by some "judgmental activity," but by the ideal unity of what is aimed at in the meaningful designation. This unity is the same each time the meaning act is renewed, whatever words are used, whatever voice utters it, whatever ink puts it on paper. What the symbol means is not some individual trait of our lived-through experience, not some recurring quality, not some property, as Husserl puts it, "of reappearing identically to itself," for we are in the presence of an ideal content presenting itself through the symbol as a unity of meaning.

But one must go further, if one is not to reduce the act of meaning to a mere intentional aiming. How conceive this passing of the aim over into a significant fullness, where it becomes embodied? Should we follow the Husserlian analyses to the letter and concede a supplementary act of meaning, that which the Sixth of the *Logical Investigations* calls an "act of fulfillment"? That is at bottom merely to baptize the problem, to give it a status within the activity of consciousness, but not to find a foundation.

No doubt that is what Husserl sensed in the revision (*Umarbeitung*) of the Sixth Logical Investigation which he prepared in 1914.[11] Through this text one can glimpse what a phenomenology of meaning might be. One and the same feature characterizes a symbol (such as a mathematical sign), a word, or an image, whether the word or the symbol be uttered or written, whether we abandon ourselves to the train of discourse or to the imagination's dreaming; something new arises outside us, a little different from what we expected, by virtue of the resistance offered by imaginary material, verbal or symbolic, and also by virtue of the implications offered by the thing now constituted as significant: by fulfilling itself in the actuality of the signifying, the intentionally virtual opens upon new virtualities. This actuality in effect is located in a spatio-temporal context, the words are inscribed in our surrounding world and point to speakers at the horizon of the verbal implications. Here is where we grasp the meaning act itself in its paradoxical nature; a taking-up of an objective theme presents itself, like a word, as a cultural object; or like an image, it presents itself as a quasi-perception. The meaning act operates as a thematic activity in which the "I speak" or the "I imagine" are brought to light. Word and image are conjugated in the first person at the very moment that they achieve objective form. No doubt this is what Husserl meant when he wrote about language:

> One thing is certain...The signified takes part in the accomplishing of the deed. He who speaks engenders not only the word, but the expression in its totality.[12]

It is finally the expressive act itself that a phenomenological analysis brings to light beneath the multiplicity of structures of signification.

This seems to us essential in a number of ways. Contrary to the traditional interpretation, the theory of signification does not seem to us to be the last word of the Husserlian eidetic of consciousness. In fact, it culminates in a theory of expression which remains cloaked, but for which the need is nonetheless present the whole length of the analyses. One might be surprised that phenomenology never developed in the direction of a theory of expression, which it left in the shadows, while bringing into full light a theory of signification. But a philosophy of expression is no doubt possible only by going beyond phenomenology.

At the moment, one thing should be noticed. This entire phenomenological analysis which we have sketched, following Husserl, calls for a completely different parsing of psychoanalysis with regard to the fact of symbolism. It would establish in effect an essential distinction between the structure of objective indication and that of signifying acts; or, to stretch things a trifle, it would place the greatest possible distance between what pertains to symptomatology and what pertains to semantics.

Psychoanalysis, by contrast, has always confounded the two structures, defining meaning by cross-referencing of objective signs and coincidences within the deciphering process. As a result, Freudian analysis could see only an artificial connection between meaning and expression, namely, the hallucinatory nature of the satisfaction of desire. Phenomenology, on the contrary, enables one to recapture the meaning in the context of the expressive act which founds it. To that extent, a phenomenological description can make manifest the presence of meaning in an imaginary content.

Thus reinstated in its expressive base, however, the act of meaning is cut off from any form of objective indication. No external context can restore it to its truth. The time and space it bears are but a furrow which immediately disappears; and others are implicated at the horizon of the expressive act only in an ideal manner, with no possibility of real encounter. To understand something or someone is thus definable in phenomenology only as a new grasp in the mode of interiority, a new way of inhabiting the expressive act, a method for reinstating oneself within it, never an attempt to situate it in its own right. This cognitive problem becomes central in any psychology of meaning and lies at the heart of any psychopathology. Along the lines of pure phenomenology, there is no principle for solving it. Jaspers, more than anyone, was troubled by this impossibility. Just to the extent that he opposed significational (*sinnhaft*) forms to sensible (*sinnlich*) forms,[13] attributing to the former alone the possibility of valid comprehension, he managed to justify the doctor-patient relationship only by a mystique of communication.[14]

Phenomenology has succeeded in making images speak; but it has given no one the possibility of understanding their language.

One would not be much off the mark in defining this problem as one of the major themes of existential analysis.

Phenomenology has indeed thrown light on the expressive foundation of all meanings; but the need to justify comprehension implies a reintegration of the moment of objective indication on which Freudian analysis had dwelt.

*

To find the foundation common to objective structures of indication, significant ensembles, and acts of expression, such is the problem posed by the twofold tradition of phenomenology and psychoanalysis. From the confrontation between Husserl and Freud has emerged a double problematic: a method of interpretation is needed that reinstates acts of expression in their fullness. The hermeneutic journey should not stop at the verbal sequences which have preoccupied psychoanalysis. It should continue to the decisive movement in which expression objectifies itself in the essential structures of indication. Much more than verification was needed: a foundation was required.

This fundamental moment in which meanings are knit together is what Binswanger tried to bring to light in "Dream and Existence."

We will be reproached for having not only gone beyond the letter of the Husserlian and Freudian texts in this presentation, but for having constructed from whole cloth a problematic that Binswanger never formulated, one whose themes are not even implicit in his texts. To our thinking, this charge carries little weight, because we are fallible enough to believe in history even when it is a question of *Existenz*. We are not concerned to present an exegesis, but to disengage an objective meaning. We believe that the work of Binswanger is important enough to bear such a meaning. That is why only its real problematic has occupied our attention. In his texts will be found the problem which he set for himself; for our part, we wanted to specify the problem to which he was responding.

III

Nihil magnum somnianti—Cicero

By bringing to light a dynamic as fundamental as dreaming and expression, Binswanger rejoined a tradition left unclarified by a 19th-century psychology that Freud did not always succeed in transcending. Psychoanalysis had inaugurated a psychology of dreams or, at least, had restored to the dream its psychological rights. And yet this was undoubtedly not to recognize its full range of validity. In Freud, the dream is the element common to the expressive forms of motivation and the method of psychological deciphering: it is at once the symbolic code of psychology and its grammar. Freud thus restored a psychological dimension to the dream, but he did not succeed in understanding it as a specific form of experience. He reconstituted the dream in its original mode with fragments of revived thoughts, symbolic translations and implicit verbalizations. The logical analysis of the whole is a logic of discourse, the motivations and structures uncovered are woven on the same psychological warp as the forms of waking consciousness. Freud psychologized the dream—and the privilege it thus acquired in the realm of psychology deprived it of any privilege as a specific form of experience.

Freud did not succeed in going beyond a solidly established postulate of 19th-century psychology: that a dream is a rhapsody of images. If it really were no more than that, a dream would be exhausted by a psychological analysis, whether in the mechanistic mode of a psychophysiology or in the manner of an investigation of significations. But a dream is without doubt quite other than a rhapsody of images, for the simple reason that a dream is an imaginary experience; and if it cannot be exhausted—as we saw earlier—by a psychological analysis, this is because it relates also to a theory of knowledge.

Until the 19th century, the problem of dreams had indeed been posed in epistemological terms. The dream had been described as an absolutely specific form of experience. If a psychology of dreams could be set forth, this had been possible only in a secondary and derivative way, on the basis of a theory of knowledge which located it as a type of experience.

In "Dream and Existence," Binswanger links up again with this forgotten tradition.

He rediscovered the notion that the signifying value of the dream tends to be tailored to the psychological analyses that can be effected. The dream experience, by contrast, has a content all the richer to the degree that it is irreducible to the psychological determinations to which one tries to adapt it. It is the old idea, so constant in the literary and mystical tradition, that only "morning dreams" have a valid meaning. "The dreams of the hale and hearty man are the morning dreams," said Schelling.[15] The idea goes back to a Greco-Roman tradition. The justification may be found in Jamblichas of Calchis: a dream cannot be deemed divine if it occurs among digestive vapors. It has value only before the meal or else after digestion, at dusk or in the morning. De Mirbel wrote in *Le prince du sommeil*: "And one must maintain the most cleansed time of night is toward morning, '*inter somnum et vigilicum*.'"[16] Théophile had one of his characters say to his Pyramus:

> The hour in which our bodies, filled with heavy vapors,
> Arouse in our senses deceitful motions
> Had already passed, and my quieted brain
> Was feeding on the poppies of sleep distilled,
> At the moment the night is about to end
> And the chariot of Dawn is yet to arrive.[17]

Consequently, the dream is not meaningful only to the extent that psychological motivations and physiological determinations intersect and cross-index in a thousand ways; on the contrary, it is rich by reason of the poverty of its objective content. It is all the more valid in that it has the less reason for being. Hence the strange privilege of morning dreams. Like the dawn they proclaim a new day, with a depth to their clarity that the wakefulness of high noon will never know.

Between the sleeping mind and the waking mind, the dreaming mind enjoys an experience which borrows from nowhere its light and its genius. Baader spoke in this sense of this "sleeping wakefulness" and this "wakeful sleep" which is tantamount to clairvoyance, and which is an immediate return to objects without passing through the mediation of the organs.[18]

But the theme of original dimensions to dream experience is not only inscribed in a literary, mystical, or popular tradition. It can easily be discerned as well in Cartesian and post-Cartesian texts.

At the point of convergence of a mystical tradition and a rationalisitic method the *Tractatus Theologico-Politicus* posed the problem of the prophetic dream. "Not only true things, but also trifles and fancies may be useful," Spinoza wrote to Boxel.[19] And in another letter, addressed to Pierre Balling,[20] on the subject of dreams, premonitions, and warnings, he distinguished two sorts of imaginings: those which depend solely on the body, its complexion and the motions of its humors, and those which give sensory body to ideas of the understanding, in which one can find at once track and sign, a tracing of truth. The one form of imagination can be found in delirium, and makes up the physiological warp of the dream. But the other makes of the imagination a specific form of knowledge. This is what the *Ethics* refers to when it shows the imagination in essential connection with the idea and with the makeup of the mind.[21] The analysis of prophetic dreams in the *Tractatus* moves at these two levels. There is the imagination tied to the motions of the body which give their individual coloring to the dreams of the prophets. Each prophet dreamed the dreams appropriate to his temperament. The affliction of Jeremiah or the anger of Elias can only be explained externally, they pertain to an examination of their bodies and the motions of their humors. But each of these dreams had its meaning, which exegesis now has the task of bringing to light. The meaning which exhibits the link of imagination to truth is the language of God to men, to show them his commandments and his truth. Men of imagination, the Hebrews understood only the Word of images. Men of passion, they could be made to submit only by the emotions conveyed in frightening and angry dreams. The prophetic dream is like an oblique path of philosophy, another experience of the same truth, "for the truth cannot contradict itself." It is God revealing Himself to men by images and figures.[22] Dream, like imagination, is the concrete form of revelation. "The prophets only perceived God's revelation by the aid of the imagination."[23]

Spinoza thereby rejoined the great classical theme of the relations between imagination and transcendence. Like Malebranche, he discovered the notion that the imagination, in its mysterious ciphers, in the imperfection of its understanding, in its half-light, in the presence which it always shows forth only elusively, points beyond the content of human experience, beyond even the discursive knowledge we can master, to the existence of a truth which surpasses man on all sides, yet bends towards him and offers itself to his mind in concrete species of images. The dream, like every imaginary experience, is thus a specific form of experience which cannot be wholly reconstituted by psychological analysis, one whose content points to man as transcended being. The imaginary, sign of transcendence; the dream, experience of this transcendence under the sign of the imaginary.

This is the lesson of classical psychology which Binswanger implicitly reaffirmed in his analysis of the dream.

*

But he also rejoined another tradition, implied in the classical one.

In the dream, as in the experience of a transcendent truth, Christian theology found shortcuts taken by divine will, a quicker way in which God may distribute His proofs, His decrees, and His warnings. It is as if a dream were an expression of that human freedom which can be inclined without being determined, which is illuminated without being constrained, and which receives warnings with something less than full evidence. In the classical literature on dreams one can detect the whole theological dispute concerning Grace, the dream standing, so to speak, to the imagination as Grace does to the heart or the will. In classical tragedy the dream is a kind of figuring forth of Grace. The tragic significance of the dream poses for the Christian consciousness of the 18th century the same problems as the theological significance of Grace. After an ominous dream, Tristan has Herod say:

> What Destiny writes cannot be erased,
> And its secret shares cannot be escaped,
> We run the more toward them
> When we think to escape them.[24]

After a dream, a character in Ferrier's *Adraste* declares:

> No, my lord, in the skies is our death inscribed,
> Man cannot cross that limit ordained,
> And measures only plunge him down
> Into the very misfortune he tries to avoid.
> Thus does the sovereign grandeur of the gods,
> Choose to play with our human weaknesses.[25]

Thus, the tragic dream for Jansenism. As for Molinism, the dream is no longer predestination, but warning or signal, more to prevent predetermination than to declare it. In Benserade's drama, Briseis says:

> Achilles, those things that mar your joy
> Are so many counsels from Heaven.[26]

In *Osman*, the lesson is even clearer:

> But heaven yet may, during our sleep,
> Turn our minds to lend us counsel,
> The outcome of our destiny
> Is not always decided by its views,
> The murmuring thunder does not always strike as lightning,
> A movement of the heart may deflect its course.[27]

But we should not be deceived. Beneath this doubtless most literary quarrel, in which from one tragedy to another the characters answer each other and throw out arguments borrowed from theological treatises, lies hidden the problem, more genuinely tragic, of destiny.

*

Man has known, since antiquity, that in dreams he encounters what he is and what he will be, what he has done and what he is going to do, discovering there the knot that ties his freedom to the necessity of the world. In the dream and its individual significance Chrysippus saw the universal concatenation of the world and the effect of *sympatheia* which conspires to form the unity of the world and which animates each fragment with the same spiritual fire. Much later the Renaissance will take up the idea again. For Campanella, it is the soul of the world—principle of universal cohesion—that inspires human instincts, desires, and dreams together. And to mark the last stage of this great mythology of the dream, this fantastic cosmogony of the dream where the whole universe seems to conspire at a momentary and vacillating image, there were also Novalis and Schelling: "The world becomes dream, the dream becomes world, and the outcome in which one believes can be seen coming from afar."[28]

What has changed from one epoch to another has not been this reading of destiny in dreams, nor even the deciphering procedures, but rather the justification of this relation of dream to world, and the way of conceiving how the truth of the world can anticipate itself and gather together its future in an image capable only of reconstituting it in a murky form.

These justifications, to be sure, are still more imaginary than philosophical, exalting myth at the boundaries between poetry and abstract reflection. In Aristotle, the value of the dream is connected with the calm of the soul, with the nocturnal dream in which the soul is removed from the agitation of the body.[29] In that silence it becomes sensitive to the most pervasive movements of the world, to the most distant agitations, and like the surface of water is all the more disturbed by the agitation at its shores as its center is the more calm and quiet; similarly, the sleeping soul is more sensitive than the waking soul to the motions of the distant world. The ripples get larger as they move and soon take on enough magnitude to make the whole surface tremble; similarly, in a dream, the weakest excitations end by distorting the whole mirror of the soul. A noise scarcely perceptible to the waking ear turns in dream into a roll of thunder, the least warmth becomes a conflagration. In the dream, the soul, freed of its body, plunges into the *kosmos*, becomes immersed in it, and mingles with its motions in a sort of aquatic union.

For others, the mythic element through which the dream joins the world is not water, but fire. In the dream, the subtle body of the soul catches fire from the secret flame of the world and thereby penetrates to the intimacy of things. This is the Stoic theme of the cohesion of the world ensured by the *pneuma* and sustained by that heat which culminates in a universal fire. It is the esoteric theme, which reached from medieval alchemy to the "prescientific" spirit of the 18th century, of an "oneiromancy," a sort of phlogiston of the soul. Finally, it is the Romantic theme in which the precise image of fire begins to attenuate, keeping only the spiritual qualities and the dynamic values; subtlety, lightness, flickering light casting shadows, ardor which transforms, consumes, and destroys, leaving only ashes where once had been brightness and joy. Novalis writes that "the dream teaches us in a remarkable fashion the subtlety with which our soul insinuates itself among objects and at the same time transforms itself into each of them."

The complementary myths of water and fire maintain the philosophic theme of the substantial unity of the soul and the world in the dreaming imagination. But one can also find other ways, in the history of dream, to justify its transcendent character. The dream may be the shadowy apperception of those things one senses all around oneself at night—or contrariwise, the instantaneous flash of light, the utter brightness of intuition, which completes itself in its very occurrence.

It was above all Baader who defined the dream by the luminosity of intuition. The dream, for him, was the lightning flash of inner vision which, beyond all sensory and discursive mediations, attains the truth in a single movement. He spoke of that "inner and objective vision" which "is not mediated by the external senses" which "we experience in our common dreams." At first, inner sensibility stands in opposition to outer sensibility, but finally, in the full grip of sleep, the former overwhelms the latter, and the mind emerges into a subjective world much more profound than the world of objects, and laden with a far weightier meaning.[30] The privilege that tradition accords to waking consciousness and its knowledge is "but uncertainty and prejudice." In the darkest night the glow of the dream is more luminous than the light of day, and the intuition borne with it is the most elevated form of knowledge.

We meet with the same idea in Carus: the dream reaches well beyond itself towards objective knowledge. It is that movement of the mind which, of its own accord, goes unto the world and finds its unity with the world. It explains in effect that waking knowledge of the world is opposition, for the receptivity of the senses and the possibility of being affected by objects are nothing but opposition to the world, "*Gegenwirken gegen eine Welt.*" The dream, by contrast, breaks down this opposition and goes beyond it—not in a luminous instant of clarity, but by the slow immersion of the mind in the night of the unconscious.

By this plunge deep into the unconscious, far more than in a state of conscious freedom, the soul will play its part in the universal intertwinings and will allow itself to be penetrated by everything spatial and temporal, as produced in the Unconscious.[31]

To that extent, the dream experience would be a *Fernsehen* like that "farsighted vision" which is limited only by the horizons of the world, an obscure exploration of that unconscious which from Leibniz and Hartmann has been conceived as the muted echo, in man, of the world in which he has been placed.

All these conceptions constitute a double polarity in the imaginary philosophy of the dream: the water-fire polarity and the darkness-light polarity. We will see later that Binswanger discovers them, empirically as it were, in the dreams of his patients. The analysis of Ellen West transcribes fantasies of soaring toward the world of light and burrowing into the cold, dark earth.[32]

It is curious indeed to see each of these themes branch out and take its place within the history of reflection on dreams, a history that seems to have exploited all the potentialities of an imaginary constellation—or perhaps imagination takes, by crystallizing them, themes constituted and brought to light by the cultural process.

Let us fasten for the moment on a single point: the dream, like every imaginary experience, is an anthropological index of transcendence; and in this transcendence it announces the world to man by making itself into a world, and by giving itself the species of light, fire, water, and darkness. In its anthropological significance, the history of the dream teaches us that it both reveals the world in its transcendence and modulates the world in its substance, playing on its material character.

We have purposely left aside until now one of the best-known aspects of the history of the dream, one of the themes most commonly exploited by its historians. There hardly exists a study of dreams, since Freud's *Interpretation of Dreams*, that does not feel obliged to cite the Tenth book of the *Republic*. One squares accounts with history thanks to Plato, and this erudite reference ensures a good conscience, as citing Quintilian does for child psychology.[33] One never fails to underline the pre-Freudian—and post-Oedipal—resonances of this famous text.

"But what sort of desires do you mean?"

"The sort that emerges in our dreams, when the reasonable and humane part of us is asleep and its control relaxed, and our bestial nature, full of food and drink, wakes and has its fling and tries to secure its own kind of satisfaction. As you know, there's nothing too bad for it and it's completely lost to all sense and shame. It doesn't shrink at the thought of intercourse with a mother or anyone else, man, beast, or god, or from murder or sacrilege. There is in fact no folly or shamelessness it will not commit."[34]

The manifesting of desire by dreams remained until the 19th century one of the most frequently used themes of medicine, literature, and philosophy. In 1613, seeking out "all the causes of dreams," André de Laurent, Physician to the King, found there movements of the humors and traits of temperament: "He who is angry dreams only of jousts, battles, fires; the phlegmatic always thinks he is in water."[35] Literature adopts authoritatively the pronouncements of the scholars. In *Mariane*, Tristan has Phérore say,

> Thus does each perceive in sleep
> The secret signs of his temperament...,

and, proceeding from the principle to examples, describes the soul of the thief who

> ...anticipating his destiny
> Encounters militia, or makes off with his loot,
> Just as the usurer in sleep runs his eyes
> And his hands over the heaps of money,
> And the lover beset already by fears or desires,
> Experiences the trials or enjoys the pleasure.[36]

Romanticism takes up the same theme and diversifies it in a thousand forms. For Novalis the dream is "the secret path" which leads to "the depths of our mind."[37] Schleiermacher discerns, in dream images, desires so vast and so deep that they cannot belong to the individual. And Bovet recalls the passage in Hugo's *Les Misérables*:

> If it were given to our bodily eyes to see into the mind of another, we would judge a man far more often by what he dreams than by what he thinks... The dream, which is all spontaneity, takes and keeps the impress of our mind. Nothing emerges more directly and with more sincerity from the very depths of our soul than our unreflective and unconfined aspirations... Our chimeras are what resemble us the most.[38]

But the closeness of these analogies should not lead us into the sin of anachronism. What is Freudian in Plato or Victor Hugo, what suggests Jung in Schleiermacher, is not of the nature of scientific anticipation. The functioning of such intuitions, and their justification, are not to be found in some unrecognized psychoanalysis. Rather, one finds, at the origin of the theme of the dream as manifestation of the soul in its inwardness, the Heraclitean principle:

> We share a world when we are awake; each sleeper is in a world of his own.[39]

Elsewhere than in "Dream and Existence," Binswanger returned several times to this principle to gauge its conceptual bearing and to bring out its anthropological significance.[40] The phrase can easily be taken in a trivial sense: the pathways of perception are closed to the dreamer, who is isolated by the internal multiplication of his images. So understood, the aphorism of Heraclitus would flatly contradict the theme, just set out, of a transcendence in dream experience, and would overlook all the sensory wealth of dream imagery, all that heat and sensible coloration which caused Landermann to say, "when we abandon ourselves to our senses, then we are in a dream."[41] What constitutes the *idios kosmos* of the dreamer is not the absence of perceptual contents but their elaboration into an isolated universe. The dream world is a world of its own, not in the sense of subjective experience defying the norms of objectivity, but in the sense that it is constituted in the original mode of a world which belongs to me, while at the same time exhibiting my solitude.

One cannot apply to the dream the classical dichotomies of immanence and transcendence, of subjectivity and objectivity. The transcendence of the dream world of which we spoke earlier cannot be defined in terms of objectivity, and it would be futile to reduce it, in the name of its "subjectivity," to a mystified form of immanence. In and by its transcendence the dream discloses the original movement by which existence, in its irreducible solitude, projects itself toward a world which constitutes itself as the setting of its history. The dream unveils, in its very principle, that ambiguity of the world which at one and the same time designates the existence projected into it and outlines itself objectively in experience. By breaking with the objectivity which fascinates waking consciousness and by reinstating the human subject in its radical freedom, the dream discloses paradoxically the movement of freedom toward the world, the point of origin from which freedom makes itself world. The cosmogony of the dream is the origination itself of existence. This movement of solitude and of originative responsibility is no doubt what Heraclitus meant by his famous phrase, "*idios kosmos.*"

*

This Heraclitean theme runs through the whole of literature and the whole of philosophy. It reappears in the various texts we have cited, which seem so close, at first glance, to psychoanalysis. But what is indicated, in reality, by this depth of the spirit, these "abysses of the soul" whose emergence is described in the dream, is not the biological equipment of the libidinal instinct; it is the originative movement of freedom, the birth of the world in the very movement of existence. Novalis, more than anyone, was close to this theme and tried ceaselessly to capture it in a mythic expression. He recognized, in the world of the dream, the reference to the existence which sustains it:

> We dream of voyages over the whole world, yet is not this whole world in us? It is in oneself and nowhere else that Eternity lies with its worlds, the past and recollections. The external world is a world of shadows and it casts its shadows on the empire of light.[42]

But the moment of the dream does not remain the equivocal instant of an ironic reduction to subjectivity. Novalis took from Herder the idea that the dream is the original moment of genesis: the dream is the primary image of poetry, and poetry, the primitive form of language, the "maternal language of man."[43] The dream is thus at the very center of becoming and objectivity. And Novalis added:

> Nature is an infinite animal, an infinite plant, an infinite mineral; and these three domains are the images of its dream.[44]

To that extent the dream experience cannot be isolated from its ethical content. Not because it may uncover secret inclinations, inadmissible desires, nor because it may release the whole flock of instincts, nor because it might, like Kant's God, "sound our hearts"; but because it restores the movement of freedom in its authentic meaning, showing how it establishes itself or alienates itelf, how it constitutes itself as radical responsibility in the world, or how it forgets itself and abandons itself to its plunge into causality. The dream is that absolute disclosure of the ethical content, the heart shown naked. This is the meaning referred to by Plato in Book Ten of the *Republic*, and not, in some pre-Freudian fashion, secret manifestations of instinct. Indeed, the wise man does not have the same dreams as the man of violence, the "tyrannical" man, governed by the tyranny of his desires and open to the political tyranny of the first Thrasymachus on the scene, the man of desire who dreams of impudence and folly. But when

> "a man of sound and disciplined character, before he goes to sleep, has awakened his reason..., has neither starved nor indulged his desires, so that they sink to rest and don't plague the higher part of him..., has calmed... his spirited element so that he goes to sleep without anger at anyone, thus going to rest with appetite and spirit quieted, while his reasoning part is stimulated, *then he is better than ever* in a state to grasp the truth in visions in his dreams undisturbed by wrong doing."[45]

Cultural history has carefully preserved this theme of the ethical value of the dream, while its premonitional import remains secondary. What the dream declares for the future of the dreamer derives only from what it discloses of the involvements and ties of his freedom. Jezebel is not there to predict imminent misfortune to Athalea: though she is told summarily that "the cruel God of the Jews has overwhelmed you," she is shown only her freedom chained down by a succession of crimes and bound over beyond appeal to the vengeance that restores justice. Two sorts of dreams are considered particularly significant: the dream of the hardened sinner who at the moment of teetering into despair sees opening before his eyes the path of salvation (sometimes the dream is transferred to someone less blind and more disposed to grasp its meaning, viz., the famous dream of St. Cecilia who can read in the dream that her son is turning to God); and the murderous dreamer who meets in the dream both the death he deals out and the death which stalks him, and who discovers the horror of an existence which has bound itself to death by a bloody pact. Linking the past to the present in the rehearsing of remorse, and knitting it into the unity of a destiny, this is the dream that fills the nights of Macbeth, and that is so frequently found in other classical tragedies.

> Pale body, immobile corpse, cold heap of bones,
> That troubleth the savor of my delights,
> Object full of horror, frightful figure
> Mingling the horrors of all Nature,
> O, come not near![46]

And Cyrano wrote in his *Agrippina*:

> The cause of my mourning
> Is the moaning sound of a fertile casket,
> A desolate shade, a speaking image,
> That tugs my garb with trembling hand,
> That sobs by the head of my bed.[47]

If the dream is the bearer of the deepest human meanings, this is not insofar as it betrays their hidden mechanisms or shows their inhuman cogs and wheels, but on the contrary, insofar as it brings to light the freedom of man in its most original form. And when, in ceaseless repetition, it declares some destiny, it is bewailing a freedom which has lost itself, an ineradicable past, and an existence fallen of its own motion into a definite determination. We will see later how Binswanger gives a new reality to this theme, ceaselessly present in literary expression, and how, in taking up again the lesson of the tragic poets, he restores, thanks to the trajectory of the dream, the whole Odyssey of human freedom.

*

Such is no doubt the meaning one must give to the *idios kosmos* of

Heraclitus. The dream world is not the inner garden of fantasy. If the dreamer meets there a world of his own, this is because he can recognize there the fact of his own destiny: he finds there the original movement of his existence and his freedom, in its achievement or in its alienation.

*

But does not the dream thus reflect a contradiction just where one might succeed in discerning the cipher of existence? Does it not designate at one and the same time the content of a transcendent world and the original movement of a freedom? The dream is deployed, we saw earlier, in a world which secretes its opaque contents and the forms of a necessity which cannot be deciphered. Yet at the same time it is free genesis, self-accomplishment, emergence of what is most individual in the individual. This contradiction is manifest in the content of the dream when it is deployed and offered to discursive interpretation. It even bursts forth as the ultimate meaning in all those dreams that are haunted by the anguish of death. Death is experienced as the supreme moment of that contradiction, which death constitutes as destiny. Hence the meaningfulness of all those dreams of violent death, of savage death, of horrified death, in which one must indeed recognize, in the final analysis, a freedom up against a world. If consciousness sleeps during sleep, existence awakens in the dream. Sleep, itself, goes toward the life that it is preparing, that it is spelling out, that it favors. If it is a seeming death, this is by a ruse of life, which does not want to die; it "plays dead," but "from fear of death." It remains of the order of life.

The dream is no accomplice of sleep. It ascends again the slope that sleep descends, towards life, it goes towards existence, and there, in full light, it sees death as the destiny of freedom. For the dream, as such, and by virtue of the meanings of existence it bears with it, kills sleep and life that falls asleep. Say not that sleep makes dreaming possible, for it is the dream that makes sleep impossible by waking it to the light of death. The dream, as with Macbeth, murders sleep.

> Sleep that knits up the ravell'd sleave of care,
> The death of each day's life, sore labour's bath,
> Balm of hurt minds, great nature's second course,
> Chief nourisher in life's feast...[48]

In the depth of his dream, what man encounters is his death, a death which in its most inauthentic form is but the brutal and bloody interruption of life, yet in its authentic form, is his very existence being accomplished.

It is doubtless no accident that Freud was halted, in his dream interpretation, by the recounting of dreams of death. They marked, in effect, an absolute limit to the biological principle of the satisfaction of desire; they showed, Freud sensed only too keenly, the need for a dialectic. But it was not in fact a matter of a rudimentary opposition of the organic and the inorganic at the heart of the dream. Freud set two external principles one against the other, one of which carried by itself all the powers of death. But death is quite another thing than one term in an opposition. It is that contradiction in which freedom, in the world and against the world, at once realizes itself and denies itself as destiny. This contradiction and this struggle may be seen in Calpurnia's dream, which foretells the death of Caesar: a dream which speaks no less of the entire power and freedom of the *imperator* who shakes the world—in the interpretation of Decius— than of the risks he runs and his imminent assassination, in Calpurnia's own interpretation.

The death glimpsed here is that which comes from behind, like a thief, to take life and tie a freedom forever to the necessity of a world. "The things that threatened me / Ne'er looked but on my back..."[49]

But death can also appear in dreams with another face: no longer that of contradiction between freedom and the world, but that in which their original unity and their new alliance is woven. Death then carries the meaning of reconciliation, and the dream in which this death figures is then the most fundamental of all: it no longer speaks of life interrupted, but of the fulfillment of existence, showing forth the moment in which life reaches its fullness in a world about to close in. Hence, in all the legends, death as reward of the wise man, as happy declaration that henceforth the perfection of his existence no longer requires the movement of his life; in announcing death, the dream exhibits the fullness of being which existence has now attained.

In this latter form, as in the former one, the dream of death appears as what existence can learn that is most fundamental about itself. In this death, anguished or serene, the dream fulfills its ultimate vocation. Nothing could be more mistaken, therefore, than the naturalistic tradition according to which sleep would be a seeming death. It is rather a matter of a dialectic of the dream itself insofar as it is a kind of explosion of life toward existence, which discovers in this light its destiny of death. The recurrence of dreams of death, which for a moment caused Freudian psychoanalysis to hesitate, the anguish which accompanies them, exhibit a death encountered, refused, cursed as a punishment, or as a contradiction. But in the serene dreams of fulfillment, there, too, is death: whether with the new visage of resurrection, for the healed man, or as the calming, at last, of life. But in every case death is the absolute meaning of the dream.

> Banquo and Donalbain! Malcolm! awake
> Shake off this downy sleep, death's counterfeit,
> And look on death itself!
> (*Macbeth*, II, iii, 79-81.)

IV

Ce qui pèse en l'homme, c'est le rêve.—Bernanos

In the filigree of the dream experience solely as transcribed in literature, philosophy, and mysticism, one can discern already an anthropological significance of the dream. This is the very significance that Binswanger
tried to retrieve from another angle, in a completely different style of
analysis, in "Dream and Existence." We do not claim either to summarize
it or to gloss it, but only to show to what extent his work can contribute
to an anthropology of the imagination. The anthropological analysis of a
dream uncovers more layers of significance than the Freudian method
implies. Psychoanalysis explores only one dimension of the dream universe, that of its symbolic vocabulary, which from beginning to end
transmutes a determining past into a present that symbolizes it. The
polysemantic character of the symbol defined by Freud as "overdetermi-
nation" doubtless complicates this scheme and gives it a wealth that reduces
the element of arbitrariness. All the same, this plurality of symbolic significations does not generate a new axis of independent meanings. Freud
sensed the limits of his analysis and perceived the need to go further.
Often he came upon signs of the dreamer situated within the oneiric drama,
as if it did not stop at symbolizing and telling in images a history of earlier
experiences, as if the dream circled about the whole existence of the
subject to restore its dramatic essence in theatrical form. Such was the
case with the second dream of Dora, whose full meaning Freud had
subsequently to admit he had not grasped.[50] Dora's dream referred not
only to her attachment to Mr. K., nor even to the actual transfer of her
feelings upon the psychoanalyst, but by way of all the signs of lesbian
fixation on Mrs. K., expressed her disgust for the virility of men, her
refusal to assume her feminine sexuality, and already exhibited murkily
her decision to put an end to this psychoanalysis which was for her only
one more sign of the grand complicity of men. Like her aphonia and her
hysterical fits of coughing, Dora's dream referred not only to the history
of her life, but to a mode of existence of which this history was, strictly
speaking, only a chronicle: an existence for which the alien sexuality of
man appeared only under the sign of hostility, constraint, irruption culminating in rape; an existence which does not even succeed in finding
itself in the sexuality so near and so parallel of a woman, but which
instead embeds its most profound meanings in rejective behavior, the most
decisive of which was to stop psychoanalysis. One could say that Dora
got better, not despite the interruption of the psychoanalysis, but because,
by deciding to break it off, she went the whole distance to that solitude
toward which until then her existence had been only an indecisive movement. All the elements of the dream point to this resolution of hers as an

active break no less than as an acceptance of solitude. Indeed, she saw herself in her dream as "going out without her parents' knowledge"; she learns of the death of her father; then she is in a forest where she meets a man but refuses to go with him; back home, she learns from the chambermaid that her mother and the others are already at the cemetery; she does not feel sad at all, goes up to her bedroom, and proceeds to read a big book.[51] Freud glimpsed this choice of solitude: beneath the explicit discourse and the dream did not Freud note the formula: "I am abandoning you and continuing my journey alone"?[52] If one cared to implicate the psychoanalyst in the psychoanalysis, surely one could not help charging Freud's failure, or at least the limitation of his understanding, to his refusal to see that this discourse was addressed to him, no less than to Mr. K.

But this is secondary. For us, the real defect of the Freudian analysis was to have discerned there one of the possible meanings of the dream, and yet to have wanted to analyze it, among others, as simply one of many semantic potentials. A method of this sort presupposes a radical objectification of the dreaming subject, which comes to play its role among other personages in a setting where it takes on a symbolic character. The subject of the dream, in Freud's sense, is always a lesser subjectivity, a delegate, so to speak, projected into an intermediate status, suspended somewhere in the play of the other, somewhere between the dreamer and what he dreams. The proof is that for Freud this dreamplay may actually represent someone else by an alienating identification; or another personage may, by a sort of heautoscopy, represent the dreamer himself.

However, it is not this quasi-subject that in fact bears the radical subjectivity of the dream experience. This is only a constituted subjectivity. The analysis of the dream ought to bring into full light the constituting feature of dream subjectivity. This is where the Freudian method becomes inadequate, for the one-dimensional meanings it extracts through the symbolic relation cannot reach this radical subjectivity. Perhaps Young understood it, he who spoke of those dreams in which the subject lives his own destiny as a dream. But it is thanks to the writings of Binswanger that one can best grasp what the dream-subject might be. This subject is not characterized as one of the possible meanings of one of the personages of the dream, but as the foundation of all its eventual meanings. To that extent, the dream-subject is not a later edition of a previous form, or an archaic stage of personality. It manifests itself as the coming-to-be and the totality of the existence itself.

*

Here is a dream analysis by Binswanger done well before the time of "Dream and Existence."[53] It concerned a young woman, age 33, who was under treatment for severe depression, with outbursts of rage and sexual inhibition. At the age of 5, she had undergone a sexual trauma. A boy had made advances; she had reacted at first with a good deal of interest and curiosity, then became defensive and violently angry. Throughout the psychotherapy she had numerous dreams. She had been in treatment for about a year when she had the following dream: she is crossing the frontier, a customs agent makes her open her luggage; "I take out all my things, the official takes them one by one, finally I take out a silver goblet, wrapped in tissue paper; then he says, 'Why do you bring me the most important thing last?'"

At the time of the dream the psychotherapy had not yet succeeded in discovering the primary trauma. When the doctor had asked the patient to associate regarding the silver goblet, she had felt a sensation of discomfort; she became agitated, her heart pounded, she felt anxious, and finally she stated that her grandmother had silver objects of this sort. She was unable to say any more, but all day she experienced a feeling of anguish which she pronounced "meaningless." Finally, that night, just as she fell asleep, the traumatic scene returned. It is her grandmother's house, she is trying to take an apple from the larder, which she had been explicitly forbidden to do. At that moment a young boy pushes the window open, enters the room, and approaches. The next day, describing this scene to her physician, she suddenly remembers that in that room, on an old harmonium no longer in use, stood a silver teapot wrapped in silver foil, and she cries: "There's the silver in the tissue paper, there's the goblet!"

At the symbolic level, granted, the dream puts the ill patient on stage. The customs inspection signifies the analytic situation in which the ill person must open her luggage and show everything she is carrying. The silver goblet relocates her in an earlier phase of her history, and shows her as in a lesser existence which scarcely belongs to her. But the essential point of the dream lies not so much in what it revives of the past as in what it declares about the future. It anticipates and announces that moment in which the patient will finally deliver to the analyst that secret which she does not yet know and which is nonetheless the heaviest burden of her present. The dream points to this secret already, down to its content, with the precision of a detailed image. The dream anticipates the moment of liberation. It is a prefiguring of history even more than an obligatory repetition of the traumatic past.

But as the subject of the dream cannot be the quasi-objectified subject of that past history, its constituting moment can only be that existence which makes itself through time, that existence in its movement toward the future. The dream is already this future making itself, the first moment of freedom freeing itself, the still secret jarring of an existence which is taking hold of itself again in the whole of its becoming.

The dream means repetition only to the extent that the repetition is precisely the experience of a temporality which opens upon the future and constitutes itself as freedom. This is the sense in which repetition may be authentic, and not by reason of its exactness. The historical correctness of a detail in the dream is only the chronicle of its authenticity. The one links together the horizontal meanings of the symbolism; the other brings to light the profound significance of the repetition. The one is oriented toward anecdotal situations, the other touches the constitutive movement of the individual's history at its source, and displays the mode of an existence as it takes shape through its temporal moments.

I do not, *I think*, distort the thought of Binswanger by interpreting in this same way the Hegelian dialectic of a dream which he sets forth in "Dream and Existence." He analyzed a dream which was dreamed by the very patient just discussed. The threefold movement of a sea, first agitated, then caught and as if fixed in a deathlike immobility, and finally, let loose in joyous freedom, is the very movement of an existence (*Existenz*) abandoned first to the chaos of a subjectivity which knows only itself, a freedom of incoherence, fantasy, and disorder; then, of a freedom invested in an objectivity which binds it to the point of overcoming it and alienating it in the silence of things dead; and finally, of a freedom rediscovered as resurrection and deliverance—but, having traversed the painful moment of objectivity in which it loses itself, a freedom that is no longer distress, cacophony, "sound and fury"; the joy of a freedom that can recognize itself in the movement of objectivity. But then we see that, if this interpretation is correct, the subject of the dream is not so much the personage who says "I" (in this case, a stroller who follows the endless shores of a beach) as the whole dream in the entirety of its dream content. The patient who is dreaming is indeed the anguished personage, but is also the sea, is also the troubling man who casts his mortal net, and is also and above all that world, first a din, then struck with immobility and death, which finally returns to the happy movement of life. The subject of the dream, the first person of the dream, is the dream itself, the whole dream. In the dream, everything says, "I", even the things and the animals, even the empty space, even objects distant and strange which populate the phantasmagoria. The dream is an existence carving itself out in barren space, shattering chaotically, exploding noisily, netting itself, a scarcely breathing animal, in the webs of death. It is the world at the dawn of its first explosion when the world is still existence itself and is not yet the universe of objectivity. To dream is not another way of experiencing another world, it is for the dreaming subject the radical way of experiencing its own world. This way of experiencing is so radical, because existence does not pronounce itself world. The dream is situated in that ultimate moment in which existence still is its world; once beyond, at the dawn of wakefulness, already it is no longer its world.

That is why the analysis of dreams is decisive for bringing to light the fundamental meanings of existence. What, then, are the most essential of these meanings?

*

They are to be found in the first movements of freedom and in its original directness. If dreams are so weighty for determining existential meanings, it is because they trace in their fundamental coordinates the trajectory of existence itself. Much has been said about the temporal pulsations of the dream, its particular rhythms, the contradictions or paradoxes of its duration. Much less about dream space.

Yet the forms of spatiality disclose in the dream the very "meaning and direction" of existence. Did not Stefan George note that "space and being-there abide only in the image" (*"Raum und Dasein bleiben nur im Bilde"*)? In lived experience, at its original level, space is not presented as the geometric structure of simultaneity. This type of space, within which the natural sciences deploy objective phenomena in their coherence, is only constituted by way of a genesis whose moments have been analyzed by Oscar Becker in their psychological aspect,[54] and by Husserl in their historical aspect.[55] Before being geometric or even geographic, space presents itself first and foremost as scene or landscape:[56] it gives itself originally as the distance of colored plenitudes or of reaches lost in the horizon, enveloped in the gathering distance; or, it is the space of things there, resistant to my touch; it is to my right or my left, behind me, opaque or transparent to my gaze. In contrast to the space of geographical reference, totally elucidated in the form of a general diagram, the scene is paradoxically closed by the infinite openness of the horizon. Everything that this horizon implies in the way of an eventual beyond delimits the familiarity of the hither and of all the pathways staked out by habit. It refers thus to the absolute of a situation which gathers in all the affective powers of the hearth, the native land, the *Heimat*. And each of these lines, which vanish into the horizon, is already like a road of return, a familiar bearing for rediscovering *ten hodou oikade*, the homeward road. In geographic space, motion is nothing but displacement: a concerted change of position from one point to another according to a previously established trajectory. The path is thus no more than the indispensable intermediary, reduced as far as possible, the lower limit of time which is indispensable for going from one point to another. In lived space, the displacement preserves an original spatial character; it does not cross, it travels along; until the very moment it stops, it remains a proffered trajectory of which only its point of departure is known for certain; its future is not prearranged by the geography of the setting, but is awaited in its authentic historicity. Finally it is the space of encounters; not merely the intersection of lines which trace the shortest distance between two points, but overlapping of journeys, paths crossing, roads which converge to the same place on the horizon, or which, like Guermantes Way, suddenly arrive, after the widest turn, at a birthplace. The dream deploys itself in this original spatiality of the scene and finds there its principal affective meanings.

"*L'espace signe de ma puissance.*" ("Space, sign of my power.") This is true of lived space only to the extent that the values of this space are reciprocally ordered. The security that space provides, the solid support that it lends to my powers, rests on the articulation of near space and far space: the latter, by which one withdraws and eludes, or which one sets out to explore or conquer; the former, that of rest, of familiarity, that which is right at hand. But this relation is disturbed in some experiences: then, far space may press upon near space, permeating it on all sides with a massive presence, with a kind of grip that one cannot loosen. Now the distant may slowly enter into the porous presence of near space, mingling with it, to the complete elimination of perspective, as in those catatonics who are "in attendance" before what is going on "around them," indifferent, as if everything were far off, yet concerned, as if everything were close, confounding the objective displacement of things at the horizon and their own bodily movement. Now, far space may penetrate the immediate sphere of the subject like a meteor—witness the patient reported by Binswanger:[57] he is properly oriented in space, but lying in bed he has the sensation that a piece of the railroad track, over there, below the window, separates from the horizon, penetrates the bedroom, traverses it, bores through his skull and lodges in his brain. In all these metatheses of the near and the far, space loses its secure character, becomes filled with stifling threats and sudden dangers, is furrowed by irruptive forces. Space, sign of my weakness.

The polarity of light and dark is not identical with that of near and far, even though they are not always distinct. Minkowski has described that dark space where hallucinatory voices cross and mingle, at once far and near.[58] In that dark world, spatial implication does not reflect the laws of juxtaposition, but the special modalities of envelopment or fusion. Space then ceases to function as a divider, no longer dissociates; it is no more than moving of shapes and sounds, coming and going according to the flux and reflux of their apparition. Over against this nocturnal spatiality one can, like Minkowski, analyze the clear space which takes shape before the subject, a levelled and socialized space where I experience in the mode of action all my potentials of movement, and where everything has its particular place, according to its function and its use. In fact, even more radically opposed to the space of darkness is a space of pure luminosity, where all dimensions seem both to be realized and to be eliminated, where all things seem to find unity, not in a fusion of fleeting appearances but in the clarity of a presence completely open to our gaze. Experiences of this sort have been described by Rümke.[59] One of his patients feels something in her so vast, so peaceful, an immense expanse of water, and feels herself dispersed in this luminous transparency. Another patient said,

> at certain times everything I saw took on enormous proportions, men
> seemed to be giants, all objects and all distances appeared to me as if
> through a magnifying lens, it would be as if I were looking through a
> pair of gloves, with more perspective, more depth, and more clarity to
> everything.

Finally, Binswanger himself analyzed the vertical axis of space in its existential meaning: the theme of the slow, raw power of enthusiasm, of joy; the theme of the glittering peak where the light mingled with shadow is purified into an absolute brightness, whose movement is fulfilled and comes to rest in the serenity of the movement. But upward movement does not imply only an existence transcending itself in enthusiasm. It is not only the direction of that selfsurpassing by which man, torn from himself, accedes, according to Fink, to "the greatest being," to the "*the-ion*".[60] The vertical axis can also be the vector of an existence that has lost its place on earth and, like Solness the Builder, is going to resume, up above, its dialogue with God. Then it indicates flight into excess, and from the start is marked by the vertigo of a fall ("he dare not, he cannot, climb as high as he builds"). And yet he is summoned from above, by the one who has burned down his house and stolen his children, by the one who wanted him "to attach himself to nothing but Him." It was toward Him that he wanted to ascend, to show Him that he would go down again, at last, to the love of man. But from such summits, one returns only in a vertiginous fall.

This set of oppositions defines the essential dimensions of existence. They form the primitive coordinates of the dream and, as it were, the mythic space of its cosmogony. In the analyses of dreams, fantasies, and deliriums, one sees them all combining and symbolizing each other to constitute a universe.

In his study of a schizophrenic, the case of Ellen West,[61] Binswanger brought out these great imaginary ensembles, whose phenomenological meanings are the precursors of the concrete, singular images that give them an expressive content. The world of Ellen West is divided between two cosmic powers that know no possible reconciliation. There is the underground world of burial, symbolized by the cold dark of the tomb, which the patient resists with all her might by refusing to gain weight, grow old, or be trapped in the crudely materialistic life of her family. And there is the ethereal, luminous world, where in a single moment a totally free existence could arise, an existence without the weight of living, that would know only that transparency of love totalized in the eternity of an instant. Life has become possible for her only in the form of a flight toward that distant and lofty space of light, and the earth, in its dark closeness, holds only the imminence of death. For Ellen West, the solid space of real movement, the space where things come to be, has progressively, bit by bit, disappeared. It has become wholly reabsorbed into limits of its own, it has become its own suppression, it is exiled into the two contradictories of which it had been the unifying moment. It exists only beyond itself, both as if it did not yet exist and as if already it no longer existed. The existential space of Ellen West is that of life suppressed, at once in the desire for death and in the myth of a second birth. It already wears the sign of the suicide by which Ellen West was to attain the culmination of her existence.

*

A phenomenological analysis, however, cannot stand by itself. It must be completed and grounded. It must complete itself by elucidating the expressive act which gives a concrete shape to these original dimensions of existence. It must ground itself by elucidating that movement in which the directions of the trajectory of existence are constituted.

We shall put aside, for the moment, the analysis of expression, leaving that for another inquiry. Let us simply note a few elements that are easily specified.

Every act of expression is to be understood on the basis of its primary directions. It does not produce these *ex nihilo*, but locates itself on their trajectory, which makes it possible, as from the points of a curve, to rediscover the whole, completed movement. To this extent, there can be an anthropology of art which would in no way become psychological reductionism. One would not refer expressive structures back to unconscious motivations, but reinstate them the whole length of that line along which human freedom moves.

On this line from near space to far space we will encounter a specific form of expression: there, existence knows the dawn of triumphal departures, voyages and circumnavigations, dazzling discoveries, the siege of towns, the mesh of exile, the stubborn return, the bitterness of coming back to things unchanged and aged, the whole course of that Odyssey of existence; on those "great cloths woven of the dreamed and the real," epic expression takes shape as a basic structure of the expressive act.

Lyric expression, by contrast, is possible only in the alternation of light and darkness where existence plays itself out. By its nature—quite apart from the topic chosen or the metaphor adopted, even though either may often be significant—the lyrical is seasonal or a "*nyct hemeral*," day-blinded with night vision, night-blinded with day vision. It is at once solar and nocturnal, and in its essence, takes on the values of dawn and dusk. The lyrical does not traverse distances, it is always the others who depart. There is no return from exile, because its own land is already exile. If the lyrical can survey all the changes of the world, all its motions, if it can, itself immobile, search out in every direction, this is because it seizes everything in a play of light and shadow, in the pulsations of day and night, which tell, upon the shifting surface of things, the unchangeable truth.

Finally, the axis of tragic expression is located along the vertical axis of existence. The tragic movement is always of the order of ascent and fall. Its special mark is that privileged moment in which it completes its rise, and balances imperceptibly, still, yet oscillating, before faltering. That is why tragedy hardly needs time and space in which to extend itself, nor foreign lands, not even the surcease of the night, for it sets itself the task of manifesting the vertical transcendence of destiny.[62]

Thus, there is an anthropological basis for the characteristic structures of epic, lyric, and tragic expression. An analysis would be needed to show both the nature of the expressive act and the anthropological necessities that dominate and govern it; one could study the expressive forms of exile, of a descent into an Inferno, of the mountain, of the prison.

Let us return to the only question that can occupy us here: how are the essential directions of *Existenz*, which form the anthropological structures of its entire history, constituted?

*

The first thing to note is that the three polarities we have described do not have equal universality and the same anthropological depth. And even though each has its independent status, one at least appears more fundamental, more originative. Hence, no doubt, the fact that Binswanger, without broaching the problem of various expressive forms, has scarcely emphasized anything but the oppositions of ascent and fall. What is the anthropological privilege of this vertical dimension?

First of all, it brings out, almost nakedly, the structures of temporality. Horizontal opposition of the near and the far exhibits time only in the chronology of spatial progression. Time unfolds only between a point of departure and a point of arrival, and is wholly exhausted in the journeying; and when it renews itself, it does so in the form of repetition, return, another departure. In this existential direction, time is in its essence nostalgic. It tries to close around itself, to recommence by linking up again to its beginning. The time of the epic is circular or reiterative. In the opposition of the light and the dark, too, time is not authentic temporality, but a rhythmic time marked by oscillations, a seasonal time where absence is always a pledge of return, and death, the pledge of resurrection.

With the movement of ascent and fall, on the contrary, one can grasp temporality in its primitive meaning.

Let us return to the case of Ellen West. The whole movement of her existence channels into a phobic fear of a fall into the grave and in the delirious desire to soar into the ether, finding its gratification in the immobility of pure movement. But this orientation and its affective polarity designate the very form according to which existence temporalizes itself. The patient does not take on the future as disclosure of a fullness and anticipation of death. She already experiences death, there, inscribed in her aging body which is more burdened each day. Death for her is only the actual weight of her flesh, is but one and the same thing as the presence of her body. During the thirteen years of her illness, Ellen West lived only to flee the imminence of this death attached to her flesh. She refused to eat or to give life in any form at all to this body, which would transform into the menace of death. Whatever gives substance, continuity, and weight to this presence of the body multiplies the deadly powers that envelop it. She rejects all food, and by the same token rejects her past. She does not take up her past in the authentic form of repetition, but suppresses it by the myth of a new birth which is to erase everything she had been. However, by virtue of this making-present of death in the guise of imminent menace, the future is emptied of its fullness. It is no longer a future by which existence anticipates it own death, taking upon itself its solitude and its facticity, but a future by which existence tears itself away from everything that grounds it as finite existence. The future into which existence projects itself is not that of an existence in the world, but that of an existence above the world, an overflight, where the limits which enclose its fullness are abolished in order to accede to the pure existence of eternity. An empty eternity, to be sure, without content, a "bad eternity," as is "bad" the subjective infinity of which Hegel spoke. This temporalization of existence in Ellen West is an inauthentic one.

Indeed, it is along this vertical direction of existence, and according to the structures of temporality, that the authentic and inauthentic forms of existence can best be allocated. This self-transcendence of the existent in its temporal movement, this transcendence designated by the vertical axis of the imaginary, can be lived as a wrenching away from the bases of the existence itself. Then we see crystallizing all those themes of immortality, of survival, of pure love, of unmediated communication between minds. Or it can be lived, on the contrary, as "transcendence," as an imminent plunge from the dangerous pinnacle of the present. Then the imaginary elaborates itself into a fantastic world of disaster. The universe is but the moment of its own annihilation: this is the constitutive moment of those deliriums of "the end of the world." Temporality's movement of transcendence can likewise be covered over and hidden by a pseudo-transcendence of space. Then the vertical axis is wholly absorbed into the horizontal trajectory of existence. The future lies in the spatially distant. Existence defends itself against the menacings of death by all those obsessional rites which block the free pathways of the world with magical obstacles. One could describe a transcendence which acknowledges itself solely in the discontinuity of the moment and which declares itself only in a rupture of itself with itself: this is the sense in which Binswanger speaks of "manic existence."[63]

These varying structures of the authentic and the inauthentic enable us to see the forms of historicity of existence. When lived in the inauthentic mode, it does not become in an historical fashion. It is absorbed into the inner history of its delirium, or its duration is wholly exhausted in the becoming of things. It gives itself up entirely to an objective determinism where its original freedom is completely alienated. And in the one case, as in the other, quite of its own impetus and of itself, existence comes to inscribe itself in this determinism of its illness. The psychiatrist then sees in this state of affairs a verification of his own diagnosis, which justifies him in considering the illness as an "objective process," and the patient as an inert thing where the process is running its course according to an inner determinism. The psychiatrist forgets that it is existence itself which constitutes the natural history of the illness as an inauthentic form of its historicity, and that what he characterizes as the reality in itself of the illness is but an instantaneous snapshot of that movement of existence which grounds its historicity at the same moment in which it temporalizes itself.

One must therefore grant an absolute privilege, among all the signifying dimensions of existence, to that of ascent and fall, where alone can be discerned the temporality, the authenticity, and the historicity of existence. If one remains at the level of the other existential directions, one can never grasp existence in any but its constituted forms. One could identify situations, define structures and modes of being, one could explore the modalities of its *Menschsein*: but one must turn to the vertical dimension to grasp existence making itself, turn to the vertical dimension in that form of absolutely original presence in which *Dasein* is defined. One thereby abandons the anthropological level of reflection which analyzes man as man within his human world, and accedes to an ontological reflection which concerns the mode of being of an existence as presence to the world. Thus is the transition effected from anthropology to ontology, confirming that this is not an a priori division, but a concrete movement of reflection. It is existence itself indicating, in the fundamental direction of the imagination, its own ontological foundation.[64]

V

Le poète est aux ordres de sa nuit.—Jean Cocteau

We must reverse our familiar perspective. Strictly speaking, the dream does not point to an archaic image, a phantasm, or a hereditary myth as its constituting elements; these are not its prime matter, and they do not constitute its ultimate significance. On the contrary, every act of imagination points implicitly to the dream. The dream is not a modality of the imagination, the dream is the first condition of its possibility.

Classically, the image is always defined by reference to the real: thus locating its origin and its positivisitic truth in a traditional conception of images as residues of perception. Or else, it defines the essence of the image negatively, as in the Sartrean conception of an "imaging consciousness" that posits its object as irreal. On the one definition, as on the other, the image bears in itself, and by a natural necessity, an allusion to reality, or at least to an eventual content of perception. No doubt Sartre has amply shown that this content "is not there"; that, indeed, I aim at it insofar as it is absent; that it offers itself, from the start, as irreal; that it remains porous and docile to my magical incantations. The image of Peter is the perception of Peter invoked, but it takes place in, confines itself to, and exhausts itself in, the irreality where Peter presents himself as absent.

> At first I only want to see Peter. But my desire becomes a desire for a certain smile, for certain features. Thus it limits itself and exasperates itself at one and the same time, and the irreal object is precisely... the limitation and the exasperation of this desire. And it is but a mirage: the desire, in the imaging act, feeds on itself.[65]

In fact, we must ask whether the image does indeed, as Sartre would have it, designate—even negatively and in the mode of unreality—the real itself.

I am trying to imagine today what Peter will do when he gets such and such news. Agreed, Peter's absence surrounds and circumscribes the movement of my imagination. But that absence was already there, before I imagined; and not in some implicit way, but in the keen mode of my regret at not having seen him for a year. That absence was already present, in the very things, the familiar things which today still bear the mark of his departure. Absence precedes and colors my imagination, but it is neither the condition of its possibility nor its eidetic index. If I had seen Peter just yesterday, my imagination today would bring him too close and would burden me with too immediate a presence. To imagine Peter after a year's absence is not to confront him in a mode of unreality (that does not require imagination, the least feeling of bitterness would suffice), it is first of all to derealize myself, it is to absent myself from that world where it is no longer possible to encounter Peter. Which is not to say that I "escape to another world," nor even that I frequent the possible margins of the real world. The lines of necessity that exclude Peter are smudged, and my presence, as presence to this world, fades. I undertake to adopt once more that mode of presence in which the movement of my freedom

was not yet caught up in this world toward which it moves, where everything still denoted the constitutive possession of the world of my existence.
To imagine what Peter is doing today in some circumstance that concerns
us both is not to invoke a perception or a reality; it is primarily to try to
recapture that world where everything is still conjugated in the first person.

When in imagination I see him in his room, I do not imagine myself
peering at him through the keyhole, or watching him from the outside.
Nor is it quite right to say that I transport myself magically into his room,
where I remain invisible. To imagine is not to actualize the fable of the
little mouse, it is not to transport oneself into the world of Peter. It is to
become the world where he is: I am the letter he is reading; I conjure
myself from that look of attentive reader; I am the walls of his room that
watch him from all sides and hence do not "see" him. But I am also his
gaze and his attentiveness, his dissatisfaction or his surprise before the
letter. I am not only absolute master of what he is doing, I am what he
is doing, I am what he is. That is why imagination adds nothing new to
what I already know. Yet it would be incorrect to say that it brings nothing
and teaches me nothing. The imaginary is not to be confused with immanence, and is not even exhausted in that formal transcendence of whatever
delineates itself as irreal. The imaginary is transcendent. Not with an
"objective" transcendence (as in W. Szilasi's sense of the term), since the
moment I imagine Peter, he obeys me; each of his gestures fulfills my
expectations, and finally he even comes to see me because I want him to
do so. But the imaginary gives itself as a transcendence where, without
learning anything unknown to me, I can "recognize" my destiny. Even
in imagination, or rather, especially in imagination, I do not obey myself,
I am not my own master, for the sole reason that I prey upon myself. In
Peter's imagined return, I am not there, before him, because I am
everywhere, around him, and in him; I do not talk with him, I hold forth;
I am not with him, I "stage" him. And it is because I rediscover and
recognize myself everywhere that I can decipher in this imagining the law
of my heart, and read my destiny there: these feelings, this desire, this
drive to spoil the simplest things, necessarily means my solitariness, at
the very instant in which I try, in imagination, to dispel it. Consequently,
to imagine is not so much a behavior towards others which intends them
as quasi-presences on an essential ground of absence; it is rather to intend
oneself as a movement of freedom which makes itself world and finally
anchors itself in this world as its destiny. Through what it imagines,
therefore, consciousness aims at the original movement which discloses
itself in dreams. Thus, dreaming is not a singularly powerful and vivid
way of imagining. On the contrary, imagining is to take aim at oneself
in the moment of dreaming; it is to dream oneself dreaming.

And just as dreams of death appeared to us to disclose the ultimate
meaning of the dream, no doubt there are certain forms of imagination

which, linked to death, show with the greatest clarity what, at bottom, imagination is. In the movement of imagination it is always myself that I derealize as presence to this very world; and I experience this world (not another one, but this very one) as entirely new to my presence, as penetrated by my presence, as belonging to me as mine. Through this world, which is only the cosmogony of my existence, I can rediscover the entire trajectory of my freedom, fathom its every direction, and totalize it as the curve of a destiny. When I imagine the return of Peter, to have an image of Peter crossing the threshold is not essential; what is essential is that my presence, inclining to dreamlike ubiquity, spread itself out on this side and on that side of the doorway; find itself wholly in the thoughts of the arriving Peter and in my own thoughts as I wait, in his smile and in my pleasure, aiming at this meeting as a fulfillment. The imagination does not tend to halt the movement of existence, but to totalize it. One always imagines the decisive, the definitive, that which is thenceforward going to be closed. What we imagine is of the order of a solution, not a task. Happiness and unhappiness are inscribed in the imagination's register, not duty and virtue. This is why the major forms of imagination are aligned with suicide. Or rather, suicide appears as the absolute of imaginary behaviors: every suicidal desire is filled by that world in which I would no longer be present here, or there, but everywhere, in every sector: a world transparent to me and signifying its indebtedness to my absolute presence. Suicide is not a way of cancelling the world or myself, or the two together, but a way of rediscovering the original moment in which I make myself world, in which space is still no more than directedness of existence, and time the movement of its history.[66] To commit suicide is the ultimate mode of imagining; to try to characterize suicide in the realistic terms of supression is to doom oneself to misunderstanding it. Only an anthropology of the imagination can ground psychology and an ethics of suicide.

Let us hold on for the moment only to the notion that suicide is the ultimate myth, the "Last Judgment" of the imagination, as the dream is its genesis, its absolute origin.

Hence, one cannot define the imaginary as the inverse function, the negative index, of reality. No doubt it develops readily on the ground of absence, and the gaps and denials by which it opposes my desires are above all what refer the world back to its basis. Yet it is also through the imaginary that the original meaning of reality is disclosed. Therefore, it cannot exclude reality. At the very heart of perception it can throw into bright light the secret and hidden power at work in the most manifest forms of presence. To be sure, Peter's absence and my dismay prompt me to dream that dream in which my existence goes forth to meet Peter. But in his presence, too, before that face which today I am reduced to imagining, I can already summon up Peter in imagination, not as elsewhere or as different, but there, where he was, just as he was. This Peter who is seated there before me is not imaginary in that his actuality might have duplicated itself and might have assigned me another, virtual Peter (the Peter I hypothesize, desire, anticipate), but is imaginary in that, at this privileged moment, he is, for me, precisely himself, Peter. He it is, toward whom I go, whose encounter promises me certain satisfactions. His friendship for me is located there, somewhere, on that trajectory of my existence I am already tracing out. His friendship marks the moment in which directions will change, or where, perhaps, they will regain their initial orientation and simply run their course. To imagine Peter when I am perceiving him thus is not to have, alongside him, an image of him as older, or as in some other place and time, but to grasp once more that original movement of our existences whose precocious concurrence can make up a single world more fundamental than that system of actuality which today defines our common presence in this room. Then my perception itself, while remaining perception, becomes imaginary by the sole fact that it finds its coordinates in the directions of existence itself. Imaginary, too, my words and feelings, this conversation I am now having with Peter, this friendship. Yet not false, for all that, nor illusory. The imaginary is not a mode of unreality, but indeed a mode of actuality, a way of approaching presence obliquely to bring out its primordial dimensions.

Gaston Bachelard is absolutely right when he shows the imagination at work in the intimate recesses of perception, and the secret labor which transforms the object one is perceiving into an object of contemplation. "One understands forms by their transformation"; then, beyond the norms of objective truth, "the realism of unreality holds sway."[67] No one has better understood the dynamic work of the imagination and the incessantly vectorial nature of its movement. But should we also follow Bachelard when he shows this movement culminating in the image, and the thrust of the image installing itself of its own accord within the dynamism of the imagination?

*

On the contrary, the image does not seem to be made of the same stuff as the imagination. The image which takes shape as a crystallized form and which almost always borrows its vivacity from memory, does indeed play the part of a substitute for the reality, functioning as the *analogon* which we earlier denied to imagination. When I imagine Peter's return, or what we shall first say to each other, I do not, strictly speaking, have an image, and what bears me along is solely the movement signifying this eventual meeting—whatever it may bring, that is, in excitement or bitterness, exultation or dismay. But here is Peter, all of a sudden, "in image," in that somber attire and that lurking smile I know him by. Did this image serve to complete the movement of my imagination and fill it with what it was still lacking? Absolutely not: for I soon cease imagining. Even if it should persist for a while, this image does not fail to refer me, sooner or later, to my actual perception, to those white walls around me that exclude the presence of Peter. The image is not given at the culminating moment of imagination, but at the moment of its alteration. The image mimes the presence of Peter, the imagination goes forth to encounter him. To have an image is therefore to leave off imagining.

The image is impure, therefore, and precarious. Impure, because always of the order of the "as if." To a certain extent, it will shape itself within that movement of the imagination which reinstates the very directions of existence, but it will feign an identification of these directions with the dimensions of perceived space, and of this movement, with the mobility of the perceived object. By presenting my meeting with Peter in this very room, and a conversation of such and such words, the image enables me to elude the real task of imagination: to bring to light the significance of this encounter and the movement of my existence which bears me toward it with such invincible freedom. That is why the "as if" of the image turns the authentic freedom of the imagination into the fantasy of desire. Just as it mimes perception by way of quasi-presence, so the image mimes freedom by a quasi-satisfaction of the desire.

And by the same token the image is precarious. It completely exhausts itself in its contradictory status. On the one hand, it takes the place of imagination and of that movement which refers me back toward the origin of the constituted world; at the same time, it points to this world, constituted in the perceptual mode, as its target. That is why reflection kills the image, as perception also does, whereas the one and the other reinforce and nourish imagination. When I am perceiving this doorway, I cannot have an image of Peter passing through it; and yet this room in which I find myself, with all that is familiar about it, with all the traces it bears of my past life and my projects, may ceaselessly assist me, by its very perceptual content, in imagining what the return of Peter and his reappearance in my life would mean. The image as fixation upon a quasi-presence is but the vertigo of imagination as it turns back toward the primordial meaning of presence. The image constitutes a ruse of consciousness in order to cease imagining, the moment of discouragement in the hard labor of imagining.

*

Poetic expression is the manifest proof. It does not, indeed, find its greatest expansion where it finds the greatest number of substitutes for reality, where it invents the most duplications and metaphors, but, on the contrary, where it best restores presence to itself—where the proliferation of analogies well up, and where the metaphors by neutralizing each other, restore the depth to immediacy. The inventors of images discover similarities and hunt down metaphors. The imagination, in its true poetic function, meditates on identity. If it is true that the imagination circulates through a universe of images, it does not move to the extent that it promotes or reunites images, but to the extent that it destroys and consumes them. The imagination is in essence iconoclastic. Metaphor is the metaphysics of the image, in the sense that metaphysics is the destruction of physics. The true poet denies himself the accomplishment of desire in the image, because the freedom of imagination imposes itself on him as a task of refusal:

> While carrying out the poetic task among the freshly cleared fields of the Word in its universality, the poet—integral, avid, impressionable, and plucky—will never welcome any enterprise which might alienate that marvel which freedom in poetry is.[68]

The value of a poetic imagination is to be measured by the inner destructive power of the image.

Exactly opposite stands the morbid fantasy, and perhaps even certain crude forms of hallucination. Here, the imagination is completely enmeshed in the image. Phantasms emerge when the subject finds the free movements of its existence crushed in the presence of a quasi-perception which envelops and immobilizes it. The slightest effort of the imagination stops, and is sucked into the image as if falling into its direct contradictory. The dimension of the imaginary has collapsed. The patient is left only with the capacity to have images, images all the more forceful, all the more tightly knit as the iconoclastic imagination is alienated in them. Phantasms cannot be understood, therefore, in terms of imagination deploying itself, but only in terms of imagination disenfranchised. The aim of psychotherapy should be to free the imaginary that is trapped in the image.

Yet a difficulty arises, one which is all the more important for us since it touches upon our main theme: is the dream a rhapsody of images? If it is true that images are but the imagination alienated, deflected in its undertaking, alienated in its essence, our whole analysis of the dreaming imagination is threatened by this very fact.

But are we in fact justified in speaking of dream "images"? No doubt we become conscious of a dream only by way of images, and starting from them. Yet in themselves they are given only fragmentarily and choppily: "First I was in a forest..., then I was at home...," etc. To be sure, as everyone knows, a suddenly interrupted dream always ends on a thoroughly crystallized image.

Far from proving that the image makes up the weave of the dream, these facts show only that the image is a view-point on dream-imagination, a way for waking consciousness to retrieve its dream features. In other words, during the dream, the movement of imagination is directed toward the primary moment of existence where the original constitution of the world is achieved. Now, when trying to grasp this movement within the constituted world, waking consciousness provides it with the lines of an almost-perceived space as coordinates, and presses it towards a quasi-presence of the image. In short, the authentic current of the imagination is reversed and, against the dream itself, images are put in its place.

For the rest, the genius of Freud bears witness to this state of affairs, since he sensed clearly that the meaning of a dream was not to be sought at the level of image content. Better than anyone, he understood that the phantasmagoria of the dream hid more than it revealed, and that it was but a compromise permeated by contradictions. But the compromise is not in fact between the repressed and the censor, between the instinctive impulses and the perceptual material. It is between the authentic movement of the imaginative and its adulteration in the image. If the meaning of the dream is always beyond the images gleaned upon waking, this is not because they veil hidden forces, but because wakefulness can reach the dream only mediately, and because between waking image and dream imagination, the distance is as great as between quasi-presence in a constituted world and original presence to a world being constituted.

Analysis of a dream starting from the images supplied by waking consciousness must precisely have the goal of bridging that distance between image and imagination, or, if you will, of effecting the transcendental reduction of the imaginary.

This is the step that, in our view, Binswanger took concretely in "Dream and Existence." And it is essential that this transcendental reduction of the imaginary ultimately be one and the same thing as the passage from an anthropological analysis of dreams to an ontological analysis of the imagination. Thus is the passage from anthropology to ontology, which seems to us from the outset the major problem of the analysis of Dasein, actually accomplished.

*

We have not, of course, followed the imagination along the whole course of its movement. We have only retraced that line that connects it to the dream as to its origin and its truth. We have only followed it in its reference back to the dream by which it breaks away from images, in which it always risks alienation. But the moment of the dream is not the definitive form in which imagination takes shape. No doubt, the dream restores the imagination to its truth and gives it back the absolute meaning of its freedom. All imagination, to be authentic, must once more learn to dream, and "*ars poetica*" has no meaning unless it teaches us to break with the fascination of images and to reopen, for imagination, its path of freedom toward the dream that offers it, as its absolute truth, the "unshatterable kernel of night." But on the other side of the dream, the movement of imagination continues. Then imagination is taken up in the work of expression that gives a new meaning to truth and freedom:

> Then the poet can see how the contraries,—these punctual yet tumultuous mirages—turn out, how their immanent heritage becomes personified, poetry and truth being, as we know, synonymous.[69]

The image can then come forward again, no longer as imagination renounced, but on the contrary as its fulfillment. Purified in the fire of the dream, what in the dream was only alienation of the imaginative, becomes ashes, but the fire itself finds its fulfillment in the flame. The image is no longer image *of* something, totally projected toward an absence which it replaces; rather, it is gathered into itself and is given as the fullness of a presence, it is addressed to someone. Now, the image appears as a modality of expression, and achieves its meaning in a "style," if one may understand by that term the originative movement of the imagination when it becomes "the Visage willing to exchange."[70] But here we are already speaking in the register of history. Expression is language, work of art, the ethical; here lurk all problems of style, all historical moments whose objective becoming is constitutive of that world whose directional meanings for our existence are exhibited by the dream. Not that the dream is the truth of history. But in bringing forth that which in *Existenz* is most irreducible to history, the dream shows best the meaning it can take for a freedom that has not yet really reached its universal moment in an objective expression. This is why the dream has absolute primacy for an anthropological understanding of concrete man. The surpassing of this primacy, however, is the task that lies ahead for the real man—an ethical task and an historical necessity:

> It is doubtless the property of this man so utterly at grips with Evil, whose voracious and medullary face he knows, to transform the fabricated fact into an historical one. Our restless conviction should not denigrate it, but interrogate it, we the fervent slayers of real beings in the successive person of our chimera... Escape into one's counterpart, with all the immense promises of poetry, will perhaps one day be possible.[71]

But all this has to do with an anthropology of expression which would be more fundamental, in our view, than an anthropology of the imagination. We do not propose to outline it at this time. We only wanted to show all that Binswanger's text could bring to an anthropological study of the imaginary. What he brought to light regarding dreams is the fundamental moment where the movement of existence discovers the decisive point of bifurcation between those images in which it becomes alienated in a pathological subjectivity, and expressions in which it fulfills itself in an objective history. The imaginary is the milieu, the "element," of this choice. Therefore, by placing at the heart of imagination the meaning of the dream, one can restore the fundamental forms of existence, and one can reveal its freedom. And one can also designate its happiness and its unhappiness, since the unhappiness of existence is always writ in alienation, and happiness, in the empirical order, can only be the happiness of expression.

NOTES

1 Cf. for example, Paul Häberlin, *Der Mensch: Eine Philosophische Anthropologie*, "Vorwort" (Zürich: Schweizer Spiegel, 1941), 7-8.

2 *Ibid.*, passim.

3 Cf. K. Schneider, *Fortschritte der Neurologie, Psychiatrie und ihrer Grenzgebiete* (Stuttgart/Leipzig: Thieme), I, 145.

4 In *Neue Schweizer Rundschau* (Zürich: Fretz u. Wasmuth), IX, 1930; reprinted in Ludwig Binswanger, *Ausgewählte Vorträge und Aufsätze* (Bern: A. Francke, 1947), 74-97. English translation by Jacob Needleman, "Dream and Existence," in Needleman, *Being-in-the-World* (New York: Basic Books, 1963), 222-248.

5 *"Über Ideenflucht"* (*Schweizer Archiv für Neurologie und Psychiatrie*, XXX, 1931-1933) was the first study of psychopathology in the mode of *Dasein*-analysis.

6 James Strachey (ed), *Standard Edition of the Complete Psychological Works of Sigmund Freud* (London: Hogarth, 1953), XII (1911-1913), 36, 36n., 63-64.

7 See Edmund Husserl, *Logische Untersuchungen* (Halle: Max Niemeyer, 1922), v.II, Pt. 1, *"Untersuchung I,"* *"Ausdruck und Bedeutung,"* Ch.1, sec. 5, pp. 30-31.—*Logical Investigations* (New York: Humanities Press, 1970; trans. J.N. Findlay), I, "Investigation 1," Ch.1, Sec. 5, p. 275.

8 Translator's note: The passage in the French text reads: "L'association rappelle à la conscience des contenus en leur laissant le soin de se rattacher aux contenus donnés suivant la loi de leurs essences respectives." The original German text by Edmund Husserl reads: "Die Assoziation ruft die Inhalte nicht bloss ins Bewusstsein zurück und überlässt es ihnen, sich mit den gegebenen Inhalten zu verknüpfen, wie es das Wesen der einen und Anderen (ihre Gattungsbestimmtheit) geseztlich vorschreibt." (*Logische Untersuchungen, op.cit.*, p.29.) The English translation by J.N. Findlay reads: "Association does not merely restore contents to consciousness, and then leave it to them to combine with the contents there present, as the essence or generic nature of either may necessarily prescribe." (*Logical Investigations, op. cit.*, pp.273- 274.) (F.W.)

9 Translator's note: The passage in the French text reads: "Les actes de formulation, d'imagination, de perception, sont trop différents pour que la signification s'épuise tantôt en ceux-ci tantôt en ceux-là; nous devons préférer une conception qui attribue cette fonction de signification à un seul acte partout identique, à un acte qui soit délivré des limites de cette perception qui nous fait si souvent défaut." The original German text by Edmund Husserl reads: "Die Akte, welche mit dem Wortlaut geeinigt sind, je nachdem dieser rein symbolisch oder intuitiv, auf Grund blosser Phantasie oder realisender Wahrnehmung, bedeutsam ist, sind phänomenologisch zu sehr different, als dass wir glauben könnten, das Bedeuten spiele sich bald in jenem, welche diese Funktion des Bedeuten einem überall gleichartigen Akten zuweist, der von den Schranken der uns so oft versagten Wahrnehmung und selbst Phantasie frei ist und sich, wo der Ausdruck im eigentliche Sinne 'ausdrückt,' mit dem ausgedrückten Akte nur vereint." (*Logische*

Untersuchungen, op. cit., v.II, Pt. 2, *"Untersuchung VI,"* sec.4, pp. 15-16.) The English translation by J.N. Findlay reads: "The acts which are united with the sound of our words are phenomenologically quite different according as these words have a purely symbolic, or an intuitively fulfilled significance, or according as they have a merely fancied or a perceptually realizing basis: we cannot believe that signification is now achieved in *this* sort of act, now in *that*. We shall rather have to conceive that the function of meaning pertains in all cases to one and the same sort of act, a type of act free from the limitations of the perception or the imagination which so often fails us, and which, in all cases where an expression authentically 'expresses,' merely becomes one with the act expressed." (*Logical Investigations, op.cit.*, v. II, *"Investigation VI,"* Ch. 1, Sec. 4, p.681. (F.W.)

10 Translator's note: The passage in the French text reads: "Comme le remarque encore Husserl, si nous pensons un chiliagone, nous imaginons n'importe quel polygone ayant beaucoup de côtés."—The original German text by Edmund Husserl reads: "Ebenso denken wir ein Tausendeck und imaginieren irgendein Polygon von 'Vielen' Seite." (*Logische Untersuchungen, op. cit.*, v. II, Pt. 2, *"Untersuchung I,"* Ch. 2, Sec. 18, p. 65.)—The English translation by J.N. Findlay reads: "...we think of a chiliagon, while we imagine any polygon with 'many' sides." (*Logical Investigations, op. cit.*, v. I, *"Investigation I,"* Ch. 2, Sec. 18, p. 302.) (F.W.)

11 Edmund Husserl, *Umarbeitung* of the "Sixth Logical Investigation." Manuscript M III, 2 II 8a.

12 *Ibid.*, p.37.

13 Karl Jaspers, *Psychopathologie générale* (Paris, Alcan, 1933; tr. A. Kastler), p.230.

14 Karl Jaspers, *Philosophy* (Chicago: University of Chicago Press, 1970; tr. E.B. Ashton), v.2, pp. 47ff.

15 F.W.J. Schelling, *Werke* (ed. Otto Weiss; Munich: Biederstein, 1946), v.I, 657.

16 De Mirbel, *Le Palais du Prince de Soimmeil, ou est enseignée l'oniromancie autrement l'art de deviner par les songes.* (Lyons: L. Pavlhe, 1670).

17 Théophile de Viau (1590-1626), *Les amours tragiques de Pyrame et Thisbe* (Napoli: Edizioni Scientifiche Italiane, 1967; ed. Guido Saba), Act IV, sc. ii, 11. 852-853, p.115.

18 Franz von Baader (1765-1841), *Werke* (Leipzig: H. Bethmann, 1850-1860), I, 475.

19 See A. Wolf (ed. & tr.), *The Correspondence of Spinoza* (London: Frank Cass, 1966), "Letter 52," p. 272. (Translation by F.W.)

20 *Ibid.*, "Letter 17," p.140.

21 R.H.M. Elwes (tr.), *Chief Works of Benedict Spinoza*, v.II, (Dover), "Ethics," Pt. II, Ax. 3.

22 *Ibid.*, v. I, Ch. 1, p. 15.

23 *Ibid.*, pp. 24-25.

24 Francois Tristan L'Hermite (1601-1655), *La Mariane.* See Claude K. Abraham *et al.* (eds.), *Le théâtre complet de Tristan l'Hermite* (University, Alabama: University of Alabama Press, 1975), p.40.

25 Louis Ferrier de la Martiniere (1652-1721), *Adraste, tragédie,* in *Theatre Francois* (Paris, 1737).

26 Isaac de Benserade, *La mort d'Achille, et la dispute de ses armes, tragédie* (Paris: A. de Sammaville, 1637).

27 Tristan l'Hermite, *Osman,* Act II, sc.i, 11. 327-332. See Claude K. Abraham, *op. cit.*, p. 785.

28 F.W.J. Schelling, *Werke (op.cit.),* IV, 217.

29 Aristotle, *The Parva Naturalia* (Oxford: Clarendon Press, 1908; ed. J.A. Beare), "De Divinatione per Somnum," Ch. II, 464a.

30 Franz von Baader, *op. cit.*, IV, 135.

31 Cf. Eduard von Hartmann, *Ausgewählte Werke, Bd. 13: Die Moderne Psychologie* (Leipzig: Haacke, 1901), pp. 32-36.

32 Ludwig Binswanger, "Der Fall Ellen West," in *Schweizer Archiv für Neurologie und Psychiatrie*, v. 53 (1944), 225-277; v. 54 (1944), 69-117, 330-360; v. 55 (1945), 16-40; "The Case of Ellen West," in Rollo May (ed.) *Existence* (New York: Basic Books, 1958), 237-364.

33 Quintilian, *Institutes of Oratory* Book I.

34 Plato, *Republic* (Baltimore, Md.: Penguin, 1958; tr. H.D.P. Lee), pp. 344-345 (Steph. 371 C-D).

35 "Discours sur les maladies mélancoliques," Ch. VI.

36 Francois Tristan l'Hermite, *La Mariane* (*loc. cit.*), Act I, sc. ii, 11. 61-62, 69-79.

37 Friedrich von Hardenburg (1772-1801; pseud. Novalis), *Werke*, II, 114.

38 Quoted by Bovet, *Intern. Zeitschrift Psychanalyse*, VI, 354.

39 See Guy Davenport (tr.) *Herakleitos and Diogenes* (San Francisco: Grey Fox Press, 1979), Fragment No. 15, p.13.

40 Ludwig Binswanger, "Heraklits Auffassung der Menschen," *Die Antike*, v. XI, 1935. Also in Binswanger, *Ausgewählte Vorträge, op. cit.*, v. I.

41 Landermann, *Die Transcendenz des Erkennens*.

42 Friedrich von Hardenburg, *op.cit.*, II, 114.

43 Johann G. von Herder, *Ideen zur Philosophie der Geschichte der Menschheit* (Berlin: Deutscher Bibliotek, 1915).

44 Friedrich von Hardenburg, *op.cit.*, III, 253.

45 Plato, *Republic, op.cit.*, p. 345 (Steph. 571D-572A). (English translation adapted to reflect French text. F.W.)

46 Arnauld, *Agamemnon*, I,1.

47 Frédéric Lachèvre (ed.), *Les oeuvres libertines de Cyrano de Bergerac* (Paris: Librarie Ancienne Honore Champion, 1921), p. 136.

48 Shakespeare, *Macbeth*, II, ii, 36-40.

49 Shakespeare, *Julius Caesar*, II, ii, 10-11.

50 James Strachey (ed.), *op. cit.*, v.7 (1901-1905), pp. 118-119.

51 *Ibid.*, pp. 109-110 & note.

52 *Ibid.*, p. 120, n.1.

53 Ludwig Binswanger, *Wandlungen der Auffassung und Deutung des Traumes von den Griechen bis zum Gegenwart* (Berlin: Springer, 1928).

54 Oskar Becker, "Beiträge zur phänomenologischen Begründung der Geometrie und ihrer physikalischen Anwendung," in *Jahrbüch für Philosophie und Phänomenologische Forschung* (Halle: Max Niemeyer, 1923; ed. Edmund Husserl), 383-560. See Sec. 7, pp. 446-459.

55 Edmund Husserl, *The Crisis of European Sciences and Transcendental Phenomenology* (Evanston, IL: Northwestern University Press, 1970), tr. David Carr; Appendix VI, "The Origin of Geometry," pp. 353-378.

56 Erwin W. Straus, *Vom Sinn der Sinne* (Berlin: Springer, 1935). *The Primary World of the Senses* (tr. Jacob Needleman; New York: Free Press, 1963), pp. 318 *et. seq.*

57 Ludwig Binswanger, "Das Raumproblem in der Psychopathologie," in *Zeitschrift für die Neurologie*, Zürich, 1933.

58 Eugene Minkowski, "Esquisses Phénoménologiques," in *Recherches Philosophiques* (Paris: Boivin), v. IV (1934-1935), 295-313.

59 Rümke, *Zur Phänomenologie und Klinik des Glückgefühls* (Springer: 1924).

60 Eugen Fink, *Vom Wesen des Enthusiasmus* (Freiburg i. Breisgau: Verlag Dr. Hans V. Chamier, 1947), 12.

61 See n. 32, *supra*.

62 Cf. Friedrich Hebbel (1813-1863): "A strange dream: A night in which my seething imagination went to its extreme in a dream so monstrous and so overwhelming that it

occurred seven more times. I had the impression that God had stretched a rope between sky and earth, placed me on it, and proceeded to swing me. I flew up and down vertiginously. Now I was among the clouds, my hair streaming in the wind, I held on, shutting my eyes; now I was hurled so close to the ground that I could make out the yellow sand, and the little white and red pebbles, and I felt as if I could touch it with my foot. I would want to get off at that moment, but before I could do so, I felt myself propelled once again into the air, and I could only hang onto the rope to keep from falling and crashing to the ground." (Gerhard Fricke, ed., *Hebbels Tagebücher* (Leipzig: Phillipp Reclam, 1936.)

63 See n. 5, *supra*.

64 To the extent to which tragic expression is located on this vertical direction of existence, it has an ontological root that gives it an absolute privilege over other modes of expression; the latter are rather anthropological modulations.

65 Jean-Paul Sartre, *L'imaginaire* (Paris: Gallimard, 1940), p.163. (My translation.—F.W.) Cf. J.-P. Sartre, *The Psychology of Imagination* (New York: Washington Square, 1966), p. 161.

66 In certain schizophrenics, the theme of suicide is linked to the myth of rebirth.

67 Gaston Bachelard, *L'air et les songes* (Paris: Corti, 1943), p. 13.

68 René Char, *Fureur et Mystère* (Paris: Gallimard, 1948: 2nd ed.), p. 86 ("Partage Formel, XXXIII"). Translator's note: The passage in the French text reads: "Au cours de son action parmi les essarts de l'universalité du Verbe, le poète intègre, avide, impressionable et téméraire se gardera de sympathiser avec les entreprises qui aliènent le prodige de la liberté en poésie." (English translation in text supplied by Mary Ann Caws.)

69 René Char, *ibid.*, "Partage Formel, XVII," p.81. Translator's note: The passage in the French text reads: "Le poète peut alors voir les contraires,—ces mirages ponctuels et tumultueux,—aboutir, leur lignée immanente se personnifier, poésie et vérité, étant, come nous savons, synonymes." (English translation in text supplied by Mary Ann Caws.)

70 René Char, *ibid.*, "Partage Formel, XXXVII," p. 87. Translator's note: The passage in the French text reads: "Il ne dépend que de la nécessité et de votre volupté qui me créditent que j'aie ou non le Visage de l'échange." (English translation in text supplied by Mary Ann Caws.)

71 René Char, *ibid.*, "Partage Formel, LV," p.92. Translator's note: The passage in the French text reads: "Sans doute appartient-il à cet homme de fond en comble aux prises avec le mal dont il connait le visage vorace et medullaire, de transformer le fait fabuleux en fait historique. Notre conviction inquiète ne doit le dénigrer, mais l'interroger, nous fervents tueurs d'êtres réels dans la personne successive de notre chimère... L'évasion dans son semblable avec d'immenses promesses de poésie sera peut-être un jour possible." (English translation in text supplied by Mary Ann Caws.)

DREAM AND EXISTENCE

Ludwig Binswanger

Dream and Existence*

Translated by Jacob Needleman

Above all, we must keep firmly in mind what it means to be a human being.[1]

(Kierkegaard)

I

When we are in a state of deeply felt hope or expectation and what we have hoped for proves illusory, then the world—in one stroke—becomes radically "different." We are completely uprooted, and we lose our footing in the world. When this happens we say later—after we have regained our equilibrium—that it was "as though we had fallen from the clouds."[2] With such words we clothe our experience of a great disappointment in a poetic simile that arises not from the imagination of any one particular poet, but out of language itself. In this respect language is every man's spiritual homeland. For it is language that "poetizes and thinks" for all of us before any one individual brings it to the service of his own poetic and thought-provoking powers. But, now, what of this "poetic simile"? Is it a matter simply of an analogy in the logical sense, or a pictorial metaphor in the poetic sense? To think either is utterly to bypass an understanding of the inner nature of poetic similes. For this nature lies, in fact, *behind* that to which logic and contemporary theories of poetic expression refer. The nature of poetic similes lies in the deepest roots of our existence (*Existenz*) where the living, spiritual form and the living, spiritual content are still bound together. When, in a bitter disappointment, "we fall from the clouds," then we *actually* do fall. Such falling is neither purely of the body nor something (analogically or metaphorically) derived from physical falling. Our harmonious relationship with the world and the men about us suddenly suffers a staggering blow, stemming from the nature of bitter disappointment and the shock that goes with it. In such a moment our existence actually suffers, is torn from its position in the "world" and thrown back upon its own resources. Until we can again find

*This translation originally appeared in *Being-in-the-World: Selected Papers of Ludwig Binswanger*, translated with an introduction by Jacob Needleman (New York: Harper & Row, 1963, pp. 222-48; *Reprinted* London: Souvenir Press, 1975). It is reprinted by kind permission of Professor Needleman. I have slightly revised the translation and added a few notes for purposes of this special issue.

"Traum und Existenz" first appeared in the *Neue Schweizer Rundschau* (Zürich), Vol. IX (1930), pp. 673-85; 766-779, and was reprinted in Binswanger's *Ausgewählte Vorträge und Aufsätze*, Vol. I (Bern: A. Francke, 1947), pp. 74-97. (KH, *Ed.*)

a new, firm standing position in the world our whole Dasein[3] moves within the meaning matrix (*Bedeutungsrichtung*) of stumbling, sinking, and falling. If we call this general meaning matrix the "form," and the bitter disappointment the "content," we can see that in this case form and content are *one*.

There are those who do not concern themselves with man as a whole, but see only one aspect of him, as biologists do when they view man as no more than a living organism. Such observers will say that falling—the high-low vector—is rooted purely in the living structure of the organism. For, they will point out, bitter disappointment is accompanied by a deficiency of muscle tone and tension in the striated muscles so that we are apt to swoon or sink. Language, they will say, is only a reflection of this purely physical circumstance. According to this view, our falling from the clouds or the giving way of ground beneath our feet is a purely analogical or metaphorical transference of one state of affairs from the sphere of the body to that of the mind, and within the latter it is simply a picturesque form of expression without genuine content or substance, a mere *façon de parler*.

Klages' theory of expression goes deeper. But with all his emphasis on the unity of soul and body his theory is still based on the presupposition that "the psychic" manifests itself in particular spatio-temporal forms that accord with our psychophysical organization. For example, a weakly defined psyche manifests itself in weak handwriting, arrogance in our carrying our heads high. And because the psyche manifests itself in such forms, language makes use of expressions drawn from the spatial-sensory sphere to indicate psychic characteristics and processes. This view is not unconvincing. But it nevertheless presupposes agreement with Klages' underlying theory of expression, which treats the body as the manifestation of the soul and the soul, for its part, as a living body. I, for one, am far from sharing these theoretical assumptions.

My views are in line with Husserl and Heidegger's doctrine of meaning, which Löwith first saw as applicable to the particular problem of language that concerns us here. When, for example, we speak of a high and a low tower, a high and a low tone, high and low morals, high and low spirits, what is involved is not a linguistic carrying over from one sphere of Being (*Seinssphären*) to the others, but, rather, a general meaning matrix in which all particular regional spheres have an equal "share," i.e., which contains within it these same particular, specific meanings (spatial, acoustic, spiritual, psychic, etc.). Sinking or falling thus represent a general meaning matrix, a vector meaning pointing from above to below, which contains a particular existential significance "for" our Dasein, according to the "ontological existential" of, say, the extending and turning outwards of spatiality, the being-thrown of mood (*Stimmung*), or the interpretation of understanding (*Verstehen*). In bitter disappointment, the ground gives way under us or we fall from the clouds not because disappointment or shock represent, as Wundt said, an "asthenic affect" that—in the form of physical staggering, stumbling, or falling—reveals itself as a threat to the upright bodily posture and thus serves as a real physical model for poetically imaginative language. It is, rather, that language of itself, in this simile, grasps hold of a particular element lying deep within the Being of man's ontological structure—namely, the ability to be directed from above to below—and then designates this element as falling. Appeal to asthenic affect and its bodily expression need not be made. What does need to be explained is why disappointment, as such, has an asthenic character; and the answer is that in disappointment our whole existence no longer stands upon "firm," but upon "weak" legs—and, indeed, no longer even stands. For because its harmony with the world has been rent, the ground beneath its feet has been taken away, leaving it suspended and hovering. Now such hovering of our existence need not necessarily assume a downward direction; it can also signify liberation and the possibility of ascending. But if the disappointment persists as disappointment, then our hovering passes into tottering, sinking, falling. Language, the imagination of the poet, and—above all—the dream, draw from this essential ontological structure.

Though our way of thinking is not very popular among psychologists and psychiatrists, it is becoming progressively more clearly delineated in the philosophical movement to which I have just referred. From our point of view, the most questionable of the many questionable problems that have puzzled our age is that of the relation between body and soul. We do not essay a solution to this problem but, rather—by attempting to remove it from its hoary metaphysical and religious rut, by doing away with such formulations as interaction, parallelism, and identity—we wish to show that it has been erroneously conceptualized. Only then can the way lie open for the treatment of such individual problems of anthropology as that which concerns us here.

That disappointment is expressed in phrases such as "falling from the clouds" is also, of course, based on further essential connections that are grasped by language, for example, our outlook is said to be "clouded" by passionate hopes, wishes, and expectations, or we say, when we are happy, that it is like "being in heaven." But falling itself and, of course, its opposite, rising, are not themselves derivable from anything else. Here we strike bottom ontologically.[4]

This same basis for the rising and falling or our Dasein is to be found in all religious, mythical, and poetic images of the ascension of the spirit and the earthly weight or pull of the body. Thus, to cite one example, I will recall Schiller's wondrous image of the transfiguration of Heracles:

Joyous in the strange, new state of hovering,

He flows upward, and the heavy, dreamlike image
Of earthly life sinks and sinks and sinks.

[Froh des neuen, ungewohnten Schwebens,
Fliesst er aufwärts, und des Erdenlebens
Schweres Traumbild sinkt und sinkt und sinkt.]

But if we wish to say who, in fact, this *we* is who happily ascends or unhappily falls, then we find ourselves somewhat embarrassed for an answer. If we are told that this *we* simply means *we human beings* and that any further questions are redundant, then it must be replied that it is precisely here where all scientific questioning should begin; for the question as to who "we human beings" actually are has never received less of an answer than it has in our age, and today we stand again precisely within the first beginnings of a new questioning with respect to this *we*. Here, too, the answer has been given by poetry, myth, and dream rather than by science and philosophy. They, at least, have known *one* thing: that this *we*, the subject of Dasein, in no way lies openly revealed, but that it loves to conceal itself "in a thousand forms." And another thing that poetry, myth, and dream have always known is that this subject must on no account be identified with the individual body in its outward form. With respect to the rising and falling of our Dasein, for example, poets have always known that it is equally valid to express the subject, the "who" of this Dasein, by either our bodily form (or by a part or member of this form), or through any property belonging to it or anything that justifies our existence in the world, to the extent that it can serve somehow to express this rising and falling. The question as to the *who* of our Dasein cannot be answered by reference to a sensory perception of the isolated form, which remains unessential, but only by reference to something that can serve as the subject of the particular structural moment (in this case the moment of rising and falling), and this subject may well be, in its sensory aspect, an alien, external subject. It is, nevertheless, *I* who remain the primal subject of that which rises and falls. The truth value and much of the effect on us of the presentation of the subject of Dasein in myth, religion, and poetry is based on these correct ontological insights. We shall now pursue our theme by simultaneously keeping in mind the presentation of the subject of the falling, plunging, or sinking.

Despairing unto death and, in his despair, enraged with himself, Mörike's *Painter Nolten*, "very unexpectedly was shamingly reproached by one whom he dearly respected." At this he suddenly experienced "the most cruel shock" that a person can experience. Reaching this point, the poet breaks off the direct description of his hero's mental state and turns directly to the reader, who then hears himself addressed in the following way: "(In such a state) it is deathly still within you, you see your own pain like a boldly soaring bird of prey stricken by a thunderbolt and now slowly falling from the sky and sinking, half-dead, at your feet." Here the unique poet speaks, rather than language as such, though at the same time he is drawing upon an essential tendency in language—falling—in the same way that he is "being used" by the corresponding essence of the Being of man. It is just for this reason that the simile instantly "reaches" the reader and affects him so that he no longer notices it as a simile, but rather, straight away pricks up his ear convinced that: "It is I who am involved, it is I who am [or, what comes to the same thing, I who could be] the mortally stricken bird of prey."

Here, we now find ourselves on the threshold of the dream. Indeed, all that we have said up to this point applies word for word to the dream that, for its part, is nothing other than a definite mode of the Being of man.

In the above simile, my own pain—that is, something in me, a "part" of me—has become a wounded bird of prey. With this there begins the dramatizing personification that we know also as the dream's principal means of representation. Now "I" no longer fall from the clouds as an individual alone in my pain. It is, rather, my pain itself that falls at my feet as a second *dramatis persona*. This is a most outspoken expression of my ability, under certain circumstances, to "purely physically" keep my feet on the ground even as I fall and introspectively observe my own falling.

If it is true of both ancient and modern poetry, and true of dreams and myths of all ages and peoples—that again and again we find that the eagle or the falcon, the kite or the hawk, personify our existence as rising or longing to rise and as falling—this merely indicates how essential to our Dasein it is to determine itself as rising or falling. This essential tendency is, of course, not to be confused with the conscious, purposeful wish to rise, or the conscious fear of falling. No, rising and the concrete goal of rising, in order to stay with the subject, are meant here essentially unreflectively, as in fact for those few through whom humanity perpetuates itself, as Cromwell has said, that no one climbs so high "as he who does not know where he is going." These are already mirrorings or reflections in consciousness of that basic tendency. It is precisely this unreflected, or—as the psychoanalysts say—unconscious moment that, in the soaring existence of the bird of prey who, high above us, quietly draws his circles in the blue distance, strikes such a "kindred" note within us.

> Innate in each of us
> Is that pressing and rising in the heart
> When the lark, lost in the blue space above us,
> Sings its warbling song;
> When high above the towering pines
> The eagle hovers, his wings outspread,
> And when above the flatness of the earth and seas
> The crane compels himself toward home.

[Doch is es jedem eingeboren
Dass sein Gefühl hinauf und vorwärts dringt,
Wenn über uns, im blauen Raum verloren,
Ihr schmetternd Lied die Lerche singt;
Wenn über schroffen Fichtenhöhen
Der Adler ausgebreitet schwebt,
Und über Flächen, über Seen
Der Kranich nach der Heimat strebt.]

Because of this "innateness," all similes involving eagles and birds—like all genuine expressions of Dasein—are not merely formally, but substantially illuminating. In still another example from poetry, I recall Mörike uses the image of an eagle to represent the happiness of love—unreflective, soaring, and fearful of falling:

The eagle aspires aloft into the open expanse,
Its eyes drinking their fill of glittering gold;
It is not foolish enough to question
Whether or not its head may hit the heavenly vault.
And love, must it not be like the eagle?
Yet it is fearful; even fears its happiness,
For all its happiness, what is it?—an endless dare!

It is well-known that in dreams flying and falling often are manifested by the hovering and sinking of our own bodily forms. These dreams of flying and falling are sometimes thought to be connected with the physical condition, especially breathing, in which case we are dealing with so-called body-stimuli dreams, sometimes with erotic moods or purely sexual wishes. Both are possible and we do not wish to dispute either assumption, since in our case it is a matter of uncovering an a priori structure of which the body-stimuli (and body schema in general) as well as the erotic-sexual themes are special, secondary contents. In these two instances, it is necessary to find certain motives in the manifest and inner life history of the dreamer in order to understand why at this particular moment this particular "content" comes to be expressed—why, for example, the dreamer at this particular time pays attention to his breathing or why, at this particular time, he is disposed to erotic wishes or fears, etc. Only then can such a dream be understood psychologically. If the wish or fear further clothes itself in a second and third person (or becomes a drama among animals), then a psychological understanding demands, further, the most minute efforts to translate these figures back into their individual psychic urges.

In the context of a particular life-history, I have analyzed elsewhere in great detail one such dream example in which the psychic conflict is represented by the attack of an eagle on a peacefully sitting marten and the abduction of the latter by the bird of prey which takes flight into the air.[5] Here I should like merely to cite a dream, yet without analyzing it more closely, which would lead us too far afield here. It is simpler, but thoroughly uniform in its representation of thoughts of death and love, and was dreamed by one of my patients during her menstrual period.

> Right before my eyes a bird of prey attacked a white pigeon, wounded it in the head and carried it off into the air. I pursued the creature with shouts and clapping of the hands. After a long chase I succeeded in chasing the bird of prey from the pigeon. I lifted it from the ground and to my great sorrow found it was already dead.

In the example taken from Mörike's *Painter Nolten*, the rising and falling Dasein found its pictorial content in the image of a bird of prey struck by a bolt of lightning. As in the dream of the eagle and the marten, what we have here, on the other hand, is a struggle between two creatures in which one represents the aspect of victorious soaring and the other of defeated falling. And, as in the *Nolten* example, the person—stricken by the pains of a shocking disappointment—sees the dying bird of prey sinking to the ground, so here too the dreamer sees the pigeon lying dead upon the ground. In interpreting the dream it makes absolutely no difference whether the drama being played in the deadly silence of the soul is acted by the dreamer's own person or by any combination of the dreamer's own person or merely by such derivative *personae*. The theme evinced in sleep by the Dasein—that is, the "content" of the drama—is the important and decisive factor; in contrast, the cast of characters is accidental and of secondary importance. Disappointment and life in descent is quite often manifested by the image of a bird of prey transformed, after its death, into some worthless thing, or plucked clean and cast away. The following two dreams of Gottfried Keller illustrate this. (In the second volume of his biography on Keller, Ermatinger has reproduced these dreams from Keller's journals):

First dream:

January 10, 1848

> Last night I found myself in Glattfelden. The Glatt flowed shimmeringly and joyously by the house, but I saw it flowing in the distance as it really does. We stood by an open window, looking out upon the meadows. There, a mighty eagle flew back and forth through the ravine. As it flew toward the slope and settled upon a withering pine, my heart began to pound strangely. I think I was moved by joy at seeing for the first time an eagle in free flight. Then it flew close by our window and we made a point of noticing that it bore a crown upon its head and that its pinions and feathers were sharply and marvelously scalloped, as they are upon coats of arms. We sprang—my Oheim and I—to our rifles on the wall and posted ourselves behind the door. The giant bird came right in through the window and nearly filled the whole room with the breadth of his

Ludwig Binswanger

wings. We fired and upon the floor lay not an eagle, but pieces of black paper piled up in a heap. This vexed us considerably.

Second dream:

December 3

Last night I dreamed of a kite. I was looking from the windows of a house; out front were the neighbors with their children. There, coming toward us, flew an enormous, wondrously beautiful kite above the rooftops. Actually, it merely glided, for its wings were tightly closed and it seemed sick and emaciated by hunger, in that it sank lower and lower and could raise itself again only with great effort—but never as high as it was before it began to sink. The neighbors and their children shouted, made a lot of noise, and impatiently began hurling their caps at the bird in order to chase it away. It saw me and seemed—in its upward and downward movements—to want to come near me. At that I hastened to the kitchen to get some food for it. I finally found some and came hurrying back to the window. It was already lying dead upon the ground and was in the hands of a vicious little boy who ripped the magnificent feathers from the wings and threw them aside, and finally, tired of this, hurled the bird upon a dungheap. The neighbors, who had felled the bird with a stone, had, in the meantime, dispersed and gone about their business. This dream made me very sad.

If we feel ourselves into these dreams—which, in any case, their aesthetic charm invites us to do—it is possible for us to sense the pulse of Dasein, its systole and diastole, its expansion and depression, its ascension and sinking. Each of these phases seems to present a dual expression: the image and the emotional response to the image; the image of the eagle in its soaring freedom and the joy in contemplating it; the image of the pieces of black paper and the distress that goes with it; the dead, plucked kite and the accompanying sadness. But basically, the joyous image and the enjoyment of it, the sad image and the accompanying sadness are *one*—namely, an expression of one and the same ascending or descending cyclical phase. In this respect, too, what is decisive is the theme supplied by the Dasein in each such phase. Whether the Dasein experiences itself more strongly in the emotive content of the image itself or in the apparently purely reactive mood of the dreamer is, as we shall see, of secondary (i.e., clinical-diagnostic) significance. By steeping oneself in the manifest content of the dream—which, since Freud's epoch-making postulate concerning the reconstruction of latent dream thoughts, has in modern times receded all too far into the background—one learns the proper evaluation of the primal and strict interdependence of feeling and image, of being-attuned (*Gestimmtsein*) and pictorial realization. And what is true of the brief cycles whose thematic reflection we can observe in the image and mood of the dreamer, is, of course, also true of the larger and deeper rhythms of normal and pathologically manic and depressive "disattune-ment" (*Verstimmung*).

We may, however, point out in passing that the happy upward cycles of life can be realized other than in images of rising, and that the same holds true *mutatis mutandis* for the unhappy downward cycles of life. Two examples will make this clear.

Gottfried Keller's second dream has an especially charming and, for us, interesting continuation. After the words, "This dream made me very sad" he continues:

> ". . . however I was very pleased when a young maiden came and offered to sell me a large wreath of carnations. It rather puzzled me that carnations were still to be found in December and I began bargaining with her. She wanted three shillings. But I had only two shillings in my pockets and was greatly embarrassed. I asked her to give me two shillings' worth of flowers, or as many as my champagne glass—in which I usually kept flowers—would hold. Then she said, "Look, they do fit," and carefully put one carnation after the other into the slender, shining glass. I watched and began to feel that sense of well-being which always comes when we watch someone perform delicate work with ease and grace. But as she put the last carnation in place I grew anxious again. The girl then looked sweetly and subtly at me and said, "Well, look! There weren't as many as I thought and they cost only two shillings." They were not quite real, these carnations—they were of a flaming red hue and their scent was extraordinarily pleasant and intense.

Thus, after the "wondrously beautiful kite" is shorn of its plumage by the "vicious little boy," and after the rude crowds have heedlessly left the dead bird lying upon a dungheap, there burgeons forth a new wave bearing no longer the image of rising, but the image of intensely colored and fragrant flowers, a sweet, delightfully roguish girl, a brilliant, slender champagne glass—all thematically linked to a happy scene that, despite threats of embarrassment and anxiety, continues to be happy to the end. Here the wave of ascension manifests itself through an orchestration of strongly sensuous and erotic stimuli and, at the same time, through the emotions that correspond to the theme of the scenic image.

At other times the sudden change of a victoriously happy vital current into one that is fraught with anxiety is expressed by the fading or disappearance of brilliantly lit colors and by the obscuring of light and vision in general—as is so well illustrated by Goethe's dream of pheasants in *The Italian Journey.*

> Since I now feel somewhat oppressed by an overwhelming flood of good and desirable thoughts, I cannot help reminding my friends of a dream which I had about a year ago, which appeared to me to be highly significant. I dreamed that I had been sailing about in a fairly large boat and had landed on a fertile and richly cultivated island, which I knew bred the most beautiful pheasants in the world. I immediately started bargaining with the people of the island for some of these birds, and they killed and brought them to me in great numbers. They were pheasants indeed, but

> since in dreams all things are generally changed and modified, they
> seemed to have long, richly colored tails, like peacocks or rare birds of
> paradise. Bringing them to me by scores, they arranged them in the boat
> so skillfully with the head inward, the long variegated feathers of the tail
> hanging outward, as to form in the bright sunshine the most glorious
> array conceivable, and so large as scarcely to leave room enough in the
> bow and the stern for the rower and the steersman. As the boat made its
> way through the tranquil waters with this load, I named to myself the
> friends among whom I should like to distribute these variegated treasures.
> At last, arriving in a spacious harbor, I was almost lost among great and
> many-masted vessels, so I mounted deck after deck in order to discover
> a place where I might safely run my little boat ashore.
>
>   Such dreamy visions have a charm, for while they spring from our
> inner self, they possess more or less of an analogy with the rest of our
> lives and fortunes.

This dream took place and was written down about a year before
Goethe set off for Italy. Its persistence and recurrence in the dreamer's
memory affords the psychologist a clear picture of the instability and even
the threat involved in Goethe's existence at the time—a danger that, with
a sure instinct, he overcame by fleeing to Italy, to the south, to colors,
sun, to new life of heart and mind.

Let us, however, turn back to dreams of flying and floating. I should
like to illustrate by means of an example that it is often not starkly pictorial
dreams that inspire psychiatric concern, but, rather, those dreams whose
pictorial content and dramatic movement retreat before the presence of
pure emotion. It is a sign of psychic health when one's wishes and fears
are predominantly objectified by the use of dramatic images, out of which,
as we have seen, emotional content may then appear to arise. In the
following "cosmic" dream of one of our patients, emotional content is so
dominant that even the exceedingly strong objectification, the image of
the cosmos or universe, no longer suffices to bind it pictorially. Here the
patient is not a bystander of the drama, detached from his own body, nor
can he completely immerse himself in the drama. The dream reads:

> I found myself in a wondrously different world, in a great ocean where
> I floated formlessly. From afar I saw the earth and all the stars and I felt
> tremendously free and light, together with an extraordinary sense of power.

The patient himself characterized this dream as a dream of dying.
This hovering without a form, this complete dissolution of his own bodily
structure (form), is not diagnostically propitious. And the contrast between
the tremendous sense of power and the personal formlessness indicates
that at the moment a deeper disturbance exists in the patient's psychic
make-up. It is no longer part of the dream but part of the psychosis as
such when the patient speaks of the dream as a turning point in his life
and finds its emotional content so fascinating that he relives it again and

again in his daydreams, preferring this feeling to every other content of life, indeed, going so far as to attempt to actually remove himself from life. What Jeremias Gotthelf once said of his dream—"I felt the healing power of night envelop me," and "Are not dreams also benign gifts of God and must we not apply them to our spiritual growth?"— cannot be related to our dreamer. How different in style and structure is a dream such as that of our patient from this—also cosmic—dream of flying by Jean Paul:

> Sometimes it would happen that, blessedly happy and exalted in mind and body, I would fly straight up into the deep blue starry skies and sing to the vaulted heavens as I rose.

How different, too, are the wonderful, if somewhat stylized, dreams of his homeland found in the fourth volume of Gottfried Kellers' *Grünen Heinrich*. Here the dreamer seems to float above a multitude of wondrous natural forms, an exceedingly rich, enchanted forest, so that what is below him appears to be a subterranean firmament, "save that it was a green sky with stars twinkling in every possible color." Compared to this, our patient's abstract cosmic phantasy can only make us shiver and shudder. And whereas Keller anxiously saw his dreams as harbingers of a serious illness and tried in every way to remove himself from their thrall, our patient lets himself become more and more captivated by the purely subjective, aesthetic allure of his dream. In the dissolution into the most subjective part of the subjective, into the pure mood-content, the meaning of life is lost to our patient, something that he himself admits: "We are in the world in order to discover the meaning of life. But life is meaningless and therefore I seek to free myself from life so that I may return to the primal force. I do not believe in a personal life after death, but in a dissolution into the primal force." A complete despair about the meaning of life has the same significance as man's losing himself in pure subjectivity; indeed, the one is the reverse side of the other, for the meaning of life is always something transsubjective, something universal, "objective," and impersonal. But we must add that, strictly speaking, as long as man is man there can never be such a thing as a *complete* dissolution into pure subjectivity. Even our patient's longing to return to the primal force still points to the desire for an objective grounding and stance. It is only that in this case the striving is, to use a distinction of Bertholet's, fulfilled purely dynamically, or even cosmic-dynamically, rather than, say, theistic-personalistically. A thorough study of our patient's outer and inner life-history shows that this return to the primal, cosmic force corresponds to a strongly erotically tinged longing for his mother, namely, the anaclitic need to lean upon a beloved mother (something that was clearly shown in the patient's youth and acted out in reality). Here, then, a strongly subjective personalism emerges from behind an apparently purely objective dynamism, a personalism that again and again puts into question the patient's foothold in the objective and impersonal.

II

The image of a bird of prey attacking a dove or some other animal in order to tear at it or destroy it is an image known to us from ancient times. Modern man, however, must build his world in his own heart, after making himself lord and master of his own life and death; and the external world, ruled by material, economic, and technical powers, can no longer offer him a foothold. Ancient man, on the other hand, neither awake nor in dreams, knew of that primal cosmic loneliness that we have just seen exemplified in our young dreamer. Ancient man would not yet have understood the profoundly wise saying of Jeremias Gotthelf: "Think how dark the world would become if man sought to be his own sun!" The man of antiquity lived in a cosmos from which he did not flee even in his most private, secret choices, whether awake or in dreams. For "what, in the moment of decision, we experience as motives are, for the initiated, acts of the gods. In them, and not in man's bottomless emotions, is to be found the depth and primary ground of everything of great significance which transpires in man."[6] It is not that we seek today to emulate classicism, taking over for our own the completed forms of ancient Greece; for the psychologist, that would certainly be an extremely short-sighted and pedantic program. But we can, as does modern humanism, realize that the cultural history of the Greeks involves the erection of a world of forms "in which the natural laws of human nature unfold in all directions," and that in penetrating this world of forms what happens is nothing less than "the self-understanding and self-development of spiritual man in the basic structure of his being."[7] From this perspective we now wish to pursue our particular problem in more detail.

When, in Penelope's dream (*Odyssey* 19, 535-81), an eagle swoops down upon the geese and breaks their necks with his crooked beak, killing them all, neither poet nor reader thinks of this as representing subjective processes in the dreamer's psyche. The dream refers to an external event, namely, Odysseus' slaying of the suitors. (The same is true of a similar dream by Hecuba in Euripides' tragedy of the same name (68-97): a dream of a wolf attacking the hinds.) These dreams, to be sure, are poetic creations. But with the insight we have gained from psychoanalysis, we can follow the famous example of Cicero who, in writing of the prophecies of his brother Quintus (which are constantly exemplified by poetic dreams), puts these words into his mouth: "Haec, etiam si ficta sunt a poeta, non absunt tamen a consuetudine somniorum." ["These things, even if they have been made by the poet, are nevertheless not uncharacteristic of the usual form of dreams."]

More often than in the dream itself, however, we find the image of eagle and dove, eagle and goose, falcon and eagle, etc., used to betoken the propitious or unfavorable answer given by an oracle or seer about the prophetic meaning of a dream. Here, too, the image refers to an external event in the future, in accordance with the basic Greek conviction that events of the world are coordinated and predetermined in detail by *Moira* and the gods. (Cf. Heraclitus' pithy saying (B 94): "The sun will not overstep his measures; otherwise the Furies, ministers of Justice, of the iron laws of necessity, will find him out.") In *The Persians* of Aeschylus we find an example of just such an oracular pronouncement consequent upon a dream. After Xerxes has departed with intent to lay waste to the land of the Ionians, Atossa, his mother, dreams of two women, one dressed in Persian garb and the other in Dorian attire. They fall to feuding, and Xerxes yokes them both to his chariot. The one bears herself proudly, the other struggles and rends asunder the harness of the car. Xerxes is hurled to the ground and his father Darius stands by his side commiserating him. But Xerxes, when he beholds Darius, rends his garments about his limbs. Deeply disturbed by this and similar dreams, Atossa draws nigh unto Apollo's altar with incense in her hand, intending to make oblation of a sacrificial cake unto the divinities that avert evil:

> But I saw an eagle fleeing for safety to the altar of Phoebus—and from terror, my friends, I stood reft of speech. And thereupon I spied a falcon rushing at full speed with outstretched pinions and with his talons plucking at the eagle's head; while it did naught but cower and yield its body to his foe.
>
> [Smyth translation, V. 191-196.]

This image is not viewed as an image stemming either from a dream or an occurrence in the external world. This indicates the extent to which the Greek mind effaced the boundaries between the various spaces of inner experience, external world, and cult. This is due to the fact that for the Greeks the subject-source of the dream image, the subject of cosmic events, and the subject of the cultist pronouncement are one and the same: the godhead Zeus, or his direct charges, to whom he has delegated his power, either temporarily or permanently. Here, then, dream image (the image of the two women harnessed to the chariot, their quarrelling, and Xerxes' fall), the external event (falcon and eagle), and cultist significance form an inseparable unity. Where do we hear any talk of an individual subject and where, then, is the possibility of either the ontological grounding or collapse of that individual? And who can decide here whether truth is to be sought in the inwardness of subjectivity or in the outwardness of objectivity? For here all "inner" is "outer," just as all outer is inner.

It is thus of no consequence whether an oracular event follows upon a dream or bears no connection with it—just as often a dream alone, without the oracle, can express the will of the godhead.

In *The Odyssey* (XV), we find two omens of similar form occurring without being preceded by dreams:

> Even as he [Telemachus] spoke, a bird flew by on the right, an eagle, bearing in his talons a great white goose, a tame fowl from the yard, and men and women followed shouting . But the eagle drew near to them, and darted off to the right in front of the horses; and they were glad as they saw it, and the hearts in the breasts of all were cheered (160-165).

From this omen Helen interprets the future to Telemachus: even as this eagle snatched up the goose that was bred in the house, even so shall Odysseus soon return to his home and take vengeance (174-77).

In the same book (XV) of *The Odyssey*, we find an image quite similar to that which occurred in the dream cited previously:

> Even as he [Telemachus] spoke, a bird flew upon the right, a hawk, the swift messenger of Apollo. In his talons he held a dove, and was plucking her and shedding the feathers down on the ground midway between the ship and Telemachus himself (525-28).
>
> [Murray translation]

This bird, too, flying forth upon the right, is sent by the gods to signify good fortune.

We thus find no mention of rising and falling in the sense of the life-flow of a particular individual. It is, rather, the kind, the family, linked as they are by a common, predetermined fate, that ascends in prosperity or falls in misery. The individual, the species, fate and the godhead are intertwined here in one unique common space. It is, therefore, even more significant and instructive that we find in this particular space of Dasein—which differs so markedly from our own—so clear a manifestation of the partial ontological structure of rising and falling.

In place of the Neoplatonic, Christian, and Romantic contrast between inner and outer, we find in the early Greeks the opposition of night and day, darkness and light, earth and sun. Dreams belong to the sphere of night and earth; they are themselves demons, dwelling within their own particular region (*Demos* in *Homer*), and forming their own tribe (*Phylon* in Hesiod). Their mother is night (Hesiod), who is also the mother of death and sleep. Thus, the close kinship between the demons of dreams and the souls of the departed who imploringly or lamentingly appear in sleep—a *motif* that appears in Aeschylus (*Eumenides*) and Euripides (*Hecuba*), as well as in Homer (*Iliad*, 22)—acquires, in the hands of these poets, a superb artistic form and a deep psychological and aesthetic effectiveness.

It is most significant that while dreams themselves belong completely to the aspect of night in the Greek Dasein, the cultist interpretation of dreams, the oracle, was gradually withdrawn from the sphere of influence of Gaia, the old godhead of earth (and closely related to Night) (cf. the ancient delphic inspirational mantic), and was usurped by the new god, Phoebus Apollo. The dream of Atossa and the omen of falcon and eagle are not distinguished according to inner and outer, or subjective and objective events, but, rather, with regard to the close at hand, constrictive, dark, damp, and obscure realm of night, and the realm of the most awake of all gods, the sun-god Apollo, who sees and aims so clearly into the distance.

We know, however, that along with this grandly uniform religious world-view of the Greeks there was also a place for sober, empirical observation and for the scientific theory that rested upon it. But above all, we know, too, of their philosophical, metaphysical interpretation of the world as an organic structure of cosmic events linked together from the most universal down to the most individual and apparently accidental. In his polemic against prophetic dreams, Cicero cites these three conceptions as possibilities for explaining prophetic signs in dreams, and then proceeds to attack all three possibilities and, with them, the whole notion of dream prophecy—with which we, today, concur. He cites (*De divinat.* II, 60, 124) the possibility of inspiration by divine powers (*divina vis quaedam*), by "convenientia et conjunctio naturae," "quam vocant (συμπάθειαν)," and by enduring and persistent observation (*quaedam observatio constans atque diuturna*) of the coincidence of dream experiences with later actual events. The new element with which he acquaints us is the doctrine of sympathy. This, however, is a doctrine that we also find in Heraclitus, the Stoics (particularly Poseidonius), and later, in a different form, in Plotinus, and again in the important dream book of Synesius. It is the famous philosophical doctrine of the One, which, wherever we may later encounter it, is bound to recall to us the spirit of ancient Greece. There are various sub-forms of this doctrine: In Heraclitus (following K. Reinhardt's *Kosmos und Sympathie*) what is involved is a oneness of Being (in the sense of 'ἐν χαὶ πᾶν) and its divisions, discord and harmony, or, as Poseidonius later formulates it, of "matter and spirit, nature and God, the accidental and the predestined." From this we have to distinguish again the All-one or oneness (in the sense of 'ἐν τὸ πᾶν), the magical union of the forces of drawing- and calling-towards, of the open and the hidden, the cultic and philosophical evocation, of the "flow from phenomenon to phenomenon," such as we find even today in superstition, and particularly in dream superstitions of all circles of society. Whereas the religious mythology and philosophy of the early Greeks recognized only a harmonious order of cosmos and world, we find already in

Poseidonius a purely dynamistic world-view: in place of the notion of order we find the notion "of an explicative" (*erklärlich*), natural, and yet secret and mysterious force," a notion that is still reflected in much of present-day scientific and philosophical theory. Among the Greeks and the Romans, all this was mirrored in the interpretation of dreams until, upon the collapse of the old world, and as an unmistakable sign of that collapse, Petronius, the fine and free-spirited confidante of Nero, scornfully explained that it was not the institutions and commands of the gods that sent man dreams from heaven above, but that every man made them himself: "Dreams, the fleeting shadow-play that mocks the mind, issue from no temples, no heavenly power sends them, each man creates his own." (*Somnia, quae mentes ludunt volitantibus umbris, no delubra deum, nec ab aethere numina mittunt, sed sibi quisque facit [Anth. lat. 651 R]*).[8]

Just as Lucretius (*De Rerum Natura* IV, 962-1029) before him presented a highly realistic account of the relation between dream experiences and daily activities, fears, wishes, and sexual desires, so Petronius put his finger on the most important aspect of modern dream theory: "Each man creates his own!" (*"sed sibi quisque facit!"*). Here, not only the history of the problem of dreams, but history itself reveals the caesura between the ancient and the modern: the *hybris* of individuation, the all-powerful and godlike human individual rears his head. Within the context of this unnatural elevation of man in contrast to the *All* of the Greek world of forms ("in which the natural laws of man unfold in all directions"), we should glance again at our particular problem: dream and existence.

III

Who is the *Quisque* of Petronius? Can we really lay our hands on the subject of the dream or even simply on the act of dreaming? The proponents of the pure *Quisque*-theory of subjectivity forget that they have grasped only half the truth. They forget that man steers his carriage "where he wishes, but beneath the wheels there turns, unnoticed, the globe upon which he moves." This holds as true for the purely scientific-genetic conception of dreams as it does with regard to the ethical significance of the dreams, the problem of man's moral responsibility for his dreams. Freud's distinction between the Ego and the Id, Häberlin's distinction between the Ego and the "universum," Jung's distinction between the individual and the collective unconscious, Schleiermacher's distinction between the individual's consciousness and that of the species, Augustine's distinction between that which merely takes place *in* us and that which takes place *through* us—all these are expressions of the distinction between the carriage and the globe upon which it moves.

There is, however, still another such distinction—an important one—

that has played a considerable role in the history of philosophy, and has done so without anyone's recalling that it was originally connected with the distinction between dreaming and awakeness. I refer to the distinction between, on the one hand, image, feeling, subjective opinion, "doxic form" (Plato, Husserl) in general, and, on the other hand, mind, objectivity, and truth. It is this distinction, again, that is the one drawn between the *Quisque*, the individual, the isolated, the *Hekastos* of the Greeks, and the human-divine community conceived of as mediated by Logos and mutual understanding. But while for Petronius and in every epoch of enlightenment the *Quisque* stands as a completely indeterminate X behind the dream he makes, here man is something more than simply a *Quisque* (though he is that, too, to the extent that he proceeds into the world of dreams, images, and feelings). Here, the individual ceases to be a structure in a naïve realistic metaphysics, and individuality becomes a mode of human being, a type and way of being human—the mode, namely, of the possibility of a nonspiritual manner of being human. One associates this doctrine with the names—to cite only a few—of Heraclitus, Plato, Hegel, Kierkegaard, Heidegger. Here we can only take note of a few points which are important for our theme.

According to Hegel, the existence of philosophy is to be dated from the time of Heraclitus, the first in whom "the philosophical idea is to be met in its speculative form." His great idea was the shift from being to becoming, his great insight was that being and nonbeing are false abstractions and that only becoming has truth. Heraclitus thereby points to the imminence of the moment of negativity that is, at the same time, the principle of vitality. Hegel and Heraclitus also agree in their deprecation and even contempt for everything individual and isolated, and for all interest in it. To this extent, both find it "senseless" (*geistlos*) "to take conscious individuality as the sole real phenomenon of existence," for "what is contradictory therein is that its essence is the universality of spirit" (Hegel, *Phenomenology of Spirit*).

In Part I, we have already explored individuality (the individual dreamer) with reference to the universal (though, to be sure, only within a small existential segment), with reference, namely, to the picture of the happy or unhappy, harmonious or unharmonious individual life and the dream image of the bird rising or falling from the sky and even its struggle with another form of bird, or with rising, flying, hovering, sinking, and falling in general. The universal that concerned us there, the transindividual image content, is not created by each individual, yet each individual sees it in his dreams and is either drawn to it or repelled by it. The individual's images, his feelings, his mood belong to him alone, he lives completely in his own world; and being completely alone means, psychologically speaking, dreaming—whether or not there is, at the time, a physiological state of sleep or awakeness. This, indeed, was Heraclitus' criterion for distinguishing dreaming and its demarcation, from the waking life of the soul. "Those," he says (Fr. 89), "who are awake (Plural!) have *one* and the same world in common (ἕνα καὶ κοινὸν κόσμον); in sleep each one (*Hekastos*, Singular) returns to his own (world) (εἰς 'ίδιον ἀποσ-τρέφεσθαι).

Much has been written concerning Heraclitus' contrast between the communal (the *Koinón* or *Xynón*) and the singular, particular, and private (the *Idion*) (cf. especially Kurt Reinhardt's *Parmenides*). Especially instructive, however, is the relationship, in this regard, to Hegel—especially in his *History of Philosophy*. Naturally, here we can only skim over the fundamental thought (cf. also the explanation of Heraclitus' Fragment 89 which I attempted with the means of the modern psychology of thought in my book *Auffassung und Deutung des Traumes von den Griechen bis zur Gegenwart*, where I have also elucidated the double meaning of this fragment, namely, that and why we have our very own world in the dream and why we turn ourselves toward it).

After Anaxagoras, the expression for world, "cosmos," which was used by Heraclitus, signified not the (objective) world, but the (subjective) state of unification (κοινός) and dispersion ('ίδιος). For Heraclitus, what defines this unification or dispersion is the "Logos," a word that sometimes must be translated (as in Jöel, Burckhardt and others) as "word" or "discourse" and sometimes as "thought," "theory," "logical necessity," "rational, lawful relation," ("harmonious-inharmonious" world-order as in Howald). It thus refers as much to understanding as it does, so Hegel says, to making oneself understood (communication). Common to both is understanding in the sense of reflective thought (τὸ φρονέειν).[9] Although there therefore exists something in which all might find something in common and communicable, namely, the Logos, yet the many live as though they were sanctioned in having their own understanding or their own private thoughts (Fr. 2).[10] This, however, regardless of the physiological state of dreaming or wakefulness is still dreaming. The dreamers fail to notice what they do after they awaken, just as they forget what they do when asleep (Fr. 1).[11] For Heraclitus, genuine awakeness is, negatively put, the awakening from private opinion (*doxa*) and subjective belief. Put positively, it is life (and not just the life of thought!) that accords with the laws of the universal, whether this universal be called *logos, cosmos, sophia*, or whether it is considered as a combination of all of them in the sense of a rational insight into their unitary, lawful interrelation and in the sense of action according to this insight. Hegel presents this Heraclitean doctrine by saying that here Reason, Logos, becomes the judge of Truth—not, however, of truth that is second best, but, rather, of divine, universal truth: "this measure, this rhythm which penetrates through to the essence of the All" (an echo of the ancient συμπάθεια). Only insofar as we live in awareness of this interconnection—whether we call it understanding, intelligibility, or reflection—are we awake. "This form of intelligibility (*Verständigkeit*) is what we call awakeness." "If we do not stand in relation to the whole, then we are merely dreaming." Separated (from the whole), understanding loses (according to Heraclitus) the power of consciousness that it had previously, and loses (according to Hegel) the spirit as an individuation of objectivity: it is not universal in its singularity. To the extent that we participate knowingly in the divine understanding we participate in the Truth; but to the extent that we are particular and special, (ἰδιάσωμεν), we are deceived. According to Hegel, these are very great and important words:

> Nothing truer or more unprejudiced can be said about Truth. Only consciousness of the universal is consciousness of truth; but consciousness of particularity and particular action, originality which results in idiosyncracy of content or form, is untrue and evil. Error, therefore, consists solely in the particularization of thought—evil and error consist in the divorce from the universal. Most men think that their conceptions should be something special and original; precisely this is illusion.

According to Hegel, "the knowledge of something of which only I am aware" is just dreaming, and the same is true of imagination (in the sense of phantasy) and emotion, "the mode, namely, in which something is only for me, in which I have something in me *qua* this subject; no matter how exalted these emotions may appear, they are nevertheless still in me and not something separable from me." Just as the object can not be merely imaginary, not merely the product of my imagination, only if I recognize it as freely existing in itself, as one universal itself, so, too, emotion participates "in the Truth" only when I—to speak with Spinoza— have knowledge of it in the form of eternity (*sub spaecia aeternitatis*). Though this may sound too abstract, it is actually quite close to home; for in every serious mental activity, and particularly in psychoanalysis, there come moments when a man must decide whether, in pride and defiance, to cling to his private opinion—his private theater, as one patient put it—or whether to place himself in the hands of a physician, viewed as the wise mediator between the private and the communal world, between deception and truth. He must, that is, decide whether he wishes to awaken from his dream and participate in the life of the universal, in the *koinòs cósmos*. It would be rather unfortunate if our patients had to understand Heraclitus or Hegel in order to get well; but none can attain to genuine health in his innermost being unless the physician succeeds in awakening in him that little spark of spirituality that must be awake in order for such a spirit to feel the slightest breath. Goethe expressed this better, perhaps, than any of our modern psychotherapists. I recall here merely the saying that he puts into Parmenides mouth ("The Wise Men and the People"):

Go into yourself! If there you do not find

Infinity in spirit and sense,
There's nothing can help you!

It is not that with the awakening of a sense for infinity as the counter to the limitedness of particularity the individual will be relieved of his images and feelings, his wishes and hopes. These, however, will simply be removed from the context of tantalizing uneasiness, restlessness, and despair, the context of falling, sinking, descending life, to the context—not of complete peace, for that would be death—but transformed into ascending, tirelessly soaring life. This is exemplified in a dream one of my patients had after a therapy session, which shows that spirituality, once awakened, can even kindle the dream into at least an image of the universal life.

> Tired and tormented by a powerful inner unrest and uneasiness, I finally dropped off to sleep. In my dream I was walking along an endless beach where the constantly pounding surf and its never-ending restlessness brought me to despair. I longed to be able to bring the ocean to a standstill and enforce a calm upon it. Then I saw a tall man wearing a slouch hat coming toward me on the dunes. He wore a broad cape and carried a stick and a large net in his hand. One eye was hidden behind a large curl of hair which hung upon his forehead. As the man came before me, he spread out the net, captured the sea in it, and laid it before me. Startled, I looked through the meshing and discovered that the sea was slowly dying. An uncanny calm came over me and the seaweed, the animals, and the fish which were caught in the net slowly turned a ghostly brown. In tears, I threw myself at the man's feet and begged him to let the sea go free again—I knew now that unrest meant life and calm was death. Then the man tore open the net and freed the sea and within me there arose a jubilant happiness as I again heard the pounding and breaking of the waves. Then I awoke!

This is a most interesting dream in many ways. Notice the trichotomy of thesis (dreaming, tormented life in isolation), antithesis (death by total dissolution of individual life following total surrender to the overpowering objective principle of "otherness"), and synthesis (by "reclaiming objectivity in subjectivity"). The dream thus pictorially mirrors the psychoanalytic process as a progression from the individual's defiant persistence in his isolation, to the humble subjection to the (impersonal) "authority" of the doctor ("transference phase"), to the "resolution of the transference." That such a loosening of the transference bond (about which so much has been and is being written) can come about *only* as a genuine inspiration, an even more lucid spiritual awakeness in the sense ascribed to it by Heraclitus and Hegel—otherwise it is a fraud and a self-conceit—is overlooked in interpretations that are either onesidedly biological or that misguidedly view the spirit as an "enemy of life." As psychotherapists, however, we must go beyond Hegel, for we are not dealing with *objective* truth, with the congruence between thinking and Being, but with "subjective truth," as Kierkegaard would say. We are dealing with the "passion of inwardness" by virtue of which subjectivity must work itself through objectivity (the objectivity of communication, intelligibility, submission to a transsubjective norm) and out of it again (as the third phase of our dream disclosed). Only on the basis of such an insight can the psychotherapist himself turn from a dreaming to a waking spirit, so that what Kierkegaard says of Lessing might be said of him: "In neither accepting an unfree devotion nor recognizing an unfree imitation, he—himself free—enables everyone who approaches him to enter into free relation with him."

All these problems are dormant in Freud's doctrine of transference to the doctor and particularly in his theories about the resolution of the transference. And they remain dormant there because no one has yet succeeded and no one will ever succeed in deriving the human spirit from instincts (*Triebe*). These two concepts are, by their very nature, incommensurable, and it is their incommensurability that justifies the existence of both concepts, each within its own proper sphere. A deeper penetration is achieved, in this respect, by Jung's doctrine of individuation as the liberation of the self from the "false veils of the *persona* on the one hand, and the suggestive force of unconscious images on the other." But however deep the insights may be that Jung gains by seeing individuation as a "process of psychological development," here, too, the fundamental problem of individuation is concealed by the fact that the contrast between dreaming and waking, suspension in one's private world and in the common world, is not understood for what it is: the contrast between image and feeling (which always belong together) on the one hand, and intellect and spirit on the other. Since, however, this contrast is there, it cannot wholly escape an explorer such as Jung. The attempt to derive this contrast from the compensatory "function of the unconscious" and its "compensatory relation to consciousness" is unsatisfactory in that the opposition seems to disappear from the view of the fundamental problem and gets buried within problems of detail and basic concepts. This is especially true with respect to the notion of the "collective unconscious," which is both a kind of imaginative "race consciousness" in Schleiermacher's sense, *and* an ethical reference to a universal, to "the world" or "the object." It is clear that in this "collective unconscious" the contrast continues unmitigated. The same holds true for Jung's concept of the self, in which conscious and unconscious "complement" each other to form a whole, a totality. The unconscious processes compensating the conscious Ego are supposed to contain within themselves all those elements necessary for a self-regulation of the total psyche. It must be borne in mind, however, that the fundamental ethical factor, the conscience, which is hidden in that compensation, first sets the entire functional dynamism in motion, and that the total psyche is not, on the contrary, regulated by the compensation mechanism; the problem is not furthered either by shifting it from the whole to its parts. Jung's theory draws successfully from Eastern sources, from India and China, and makes good use of knowledge of primitive mentality. We, on the other hand, with all due respect to these sources, do not think it justified to step backwards—in psychology, psychoanalysis, and psychiatry—from the point attained by the Greeks in their interpretation of existence.

We now return to our point of departure. When a bitter disappointment causes the ground beneath my feet to give way, then later, after I have "pulled myself together again," I express what happened by saying, "I didn't know what hit me." To use Heidegger's words here, Dasein is brought before its own Being—insofar, that is, as something happens to it and Dasein knows neither the "how" nor the "what" of the happening. This is the basic ontological element of all dreaming and its relatedness to anxiety.[12] To dream means: I don't know what is happening to me. From the I and the Me there again emerges, to be sure, the individual, the *Quisque* and *Hekastos*; in no way, however, does the individual emerge as he who makes the dream, but rather as the one for whom—"he knows not how"—the dream occurs. And this individual is, here, none other than "the selfsame" in the sense of "personal numerical identity" (Kant): purely formal indication, without substance, it is the plaything of rising and falling life, the roar of the sea and the stillness of death, the brilliance of sun-bathed color and shadowy night, the sublime form of the eagle in flight and the chaotic heap of paper upon the floor, the splendor of a young maiden, the scent of seaweed, the corpse of a fallen bird, the powerful, terrible bird of prey, and the gentle dove. An individual turns from mere self-identity to becoming a self or "the" individual, and the dreamer awakens in that unfathomable moment when he decides not only to seek to know "what hit him," but seeks also to strike into and take hold of the dynamics in these events, "himself"—the moment, that is, when he resolves to bring continuity or consequence into a life that rises and falls, falls and rises. Only then does he *make* something. That which he makes, however, is not life—this the individual cannot make—but history. Dreaming, man—to use a distinction I have drawn elsewhere—"is" "life-function;" waking, he creates "life-history." What he actually makes is the history of his own life, his inner life-history, and we must not confuse this with participation or nonparticipation in outer or world-history, which by no means lies completely within his power. It is not possible —no matter how often the attempt is made—to reduce both parts of the disjunction between life-function and inner life-history to a common denominator, because life considered as function is not the same as life considered as history. And yet, both do have a common foundation: existence.

Our goal here has been to indicate the place of dreaming within the context of this common foundation. But even apart from this we may point out that dreaming and awakeness have something else in common. Just as the "transition" from one to the other is a gradual one (which is not affected by the leap-character of the individual life-historical decision), so the beginning of life-function (and, with it, of dreaming) and the end of inner life-history (awakeness) lie in infinity. For just as we do not know where life and the dream begin, so we are, in the course of our lives, ever again reminded that it lies beyond man's powers "to be 'the individual' in the highest sense."

NOTES

1 Søren Kierkegaard, *Concluding Unscientific Postscript*, trans. David F. Swenson and Walter Lowrie (Princeton: Princeton University Press, 1941), p. 177.

2 The idiom in German is *aus allen Himmeln fallen* (to be bitterly disappointed or utterly disillusioned) and *wie vom Himmel gefallen sein* (to be astounded). English contains many similar linkages between falling and disappointment, such as, "The ground gave way beneath my feet," "I came down to earth with a thud," and "The rug was pulled out from under me." The interesting—but for Binswanger's point unessential—difference between the two idioms is that the German locates in the sky any person with deeply felt hopes, while the English reserves this place for a person with exhorbitant or unrealistic hopes. The primary point here, however, concerns the falling itself, which is expressed by the idioms of both languages. The phrase "to fall from the clouds," which I have used here, should not, therefore, be understood as implying anything about the reasonableness of the shattered hopes. [J.N., *Trans.*]

3 *Dasein*, which literally means "Being-there," is normally translated as presence, being, or existence, and indeed usually refers to human existence. It is the term used by Heidegger in *Being and Time* (trans. John Macquarrie and Edward Robinson [New York: Harper & Row, 1962] to signify man's particular kind of Being:

> Thus to work out the question of Being adequately, we must make an entity—the inquirer—transparent in his own Being.... This entity which each of us is himself and which includes inquiring as one of the possibilities of its Being, we shall denote by the term *"Dasein."* (p. 27)

> Dasein is an entity which does not just occur among other entities. Rather, it is ontically distinguished by the fact that, in its very Being, that Being is an *issue* for it.... It is peculiar to this entity that with and through its Being, this Being is disclosed to it. *Understanding of Being is itself a definite characteristic of Dasein's Being* .... That kind of Being towards which Dasein can comport itself in one way or another, and always does comport itself somehow, we call "existence" (*Existenz*). (p. 32)

> The essence of Dasein lies in its existence. (p. 67)

Since in this 1930 essay Binswanger is clearly using the term Dasein as Heidegger has defined it in *Being and Time*, which was originally published in 1927, the term has been left untranslated, following the Heidegger literature.

4 When "Dream and Existence" was reprinted in his 1947 collection of essays (*Ausgewählte Vorträge and Aufsätze*), Binswanger left out the rest of this paragraph, which had originally appeared in the 1930 version published in the *Neue Schweizer Rundschau*. In his Preface to the selected essays, he does note this omission, although he does not offer any particular explanation for it. With the exception of the deletion of this passage

on Rilke, the 1930 and 1947 versions are identical. The missing passage reads as follows:

> Apart from the linguistic resources (*Sprachgut*) of entire peoples, we must even today still turn primarily to individual creators of language, to the poets, if we want to see something on this basis. They have a knowledge of the fact that in happiness we actually do ascend, that in disappointed hopes or in unhappiness we actually do fall, and that our Dasein does indeed cease to be a living Dasein when this foundation is turned into its opposite. Only for our departed ones may it hence have validity that even in falling there is happiness, like the "rain which falls upon the dark soil in spring;" however, it is a kind of happiness that we living ones no longer understand: for we, so sings the poet and seer, recently taken from us, in one of his most beautiful elegies,
>
> >...we, who think of happiness
> >*Ascending*, would then experience
> >The feeling which almost startles
> >When what is happy *falls*.
>
> Naturally, that does not mean that the real fall of man from the heaven of his happiness upon the earth of his unhappiness touches or amazes us; rather, the thought touches us that our departed ones, even if they could still speak to us, would speak a different language than we ourselves—a language in which below and above, rising and falling, would turn into their opposites, so that even then we could no longer understand them, and it would remain true that no step would any longer reverberate from their "soundless fate."

Rilke died in 1926. The passage makes up the last four lines of the tenth (and last) of the *Duino Elegies*. The translation of the poetry is by Ruth Speirs, *An Anthology of German Poetry from Hölderlin to Rilke in English Translation*, ed. Angel Flores (Gloucester, MA: Peter Smith, 1965), p. 466.

5 Ludwig Binswanger, *Wandlungen in der Auffasung und Deutung des Traumes von den Griechen bis zur Gegenwart* (Berlin: Springer Verlag, 1928).

6 Walter F. Otto, *Die Götter Griechenlands* (Bonn: Verlag Cohen). [L.B.]

7 Werner Jaeger, *Die geistige Gegenwart der Antike* (Berlin: Verlag de Gruyter). [L.B.]

8 Petronius, *The Satyricon* and Seneca, *The Apocolocyntosis*, trans. J. P. Sullivan (New York: Penguin Books, 1965), p. 174. In translation, Petronius' entire Fragment XXX reads:

> Dreams
> The fleeting shadow-play that mocks the mind,
> Issue from no temples,
> No heavenly power sends them—
> Each man creates his own.
> When prostrate limbs grow heavy
> And the play of the mind is unchecked,
> The mind enacts in darkness
> The dramas of daylight.
> >The shatterer of cities in war,
> >Who fires unlucky towns,
> >Sees flying spears, broken ranks, the death of kings,
> >Plains awash with spilt blood.
> >The barrister pleads again in nightmare,
> >Sees the twelve tables, the court, the guarded bench.
> >The miser salts away his money
> >To find his gold dug up.
> >The hunter flushes the woodland with his hounds.
> >The sailor dreams he is doomed,
> >Drags out of the sea the upturned poop,
> >Or clings to it.

The mistress scribbles a note to her lover;
The guilty lover sends a gift...
And the hound in his slumbers bays at the hare's tracks.
[The pangs of unhappiness last
Into the watches of the night.]

9 Concerning the central significance of φρονεῖν and φρόνησις in Greek philosophy and what they meant for Socrates, Plato, and Aristotle, see Werner Jaeger, *Aristotle*. [L.B.]

10 Although the original German text cites Heraclitus' Fragment 92 here, this is clearly a misprint. It is evident from Binswanger's paraphrase that he is referring to Fragment 2: "Therefore it is necessary to follow the common; but although the *Logos* is common, the many live as though they had a private understanding," trans. G. S. Kirk, in G. S. Kirk and J. E. Raven, *The Presocratic Philosophers* (Cambridge: Cambridge University Press, 1957), p. 188.

11 Heraclitus' Fragment 1: "Of the *Logos* which is as I describe it men always prove to be uncomprehending, both before they have heard it and when once they have heard it. For although all things happen according to this *Logos* men are like people of no experience, even when they experience such words and deeds as I explain, when I distinguish each thing according to its constitution and declare how it is; but the rest of men fail to notice what they do after they wake up just as they forget what they do when asleep," Kirk and Raven, p. 187.

For Binswanger's further thoughts on Heraclitus, *see also* his "Heraklits Auffassung des Menschen," in *Vorträge und Aufsätze*, Vol. I (Bern: A. Francke, 1947), pp. 98-131.

12 We view anxiety dreams as the prototype of the Dasein's (as such) primal essential anxiety. *See* Heidegger, *Was ist Metaphysik?* [L.B.] ["What is Metaphysics?" trans. David Farrell Krell, in *Basic Writings*, ed. D. F. Krell (New York: Harper & Row, 1977), pp. 95-112. This lecture was originally given in 1929.]

MICHEL FOUCAULT
Theoretical Traditions in the Social Sciences
Mark Cousins and Athar Hussein

''A good introduction to Foucault's main writings.''—S. Restivo, Rensselaer Polytechnic Institute, in *Choice*

''Cousins and Hussain have produced one of the better commentaries on Foucault. Their book can serve as a nice introduction to his work. It is well written and avoids the temptation to paraphrase which has proved irresistable to so many commentators. Moreover, they are willing to follow Foucault into some of the more obscure corners of his thought. Their discussion of the classic age and the Port Royal grammar is the best I've seen. Their discussion of Foucault's relation to Descartes, always an important topic in the discussion of a French author, is unique and illuminating.''—Roger Paden, in *Telos*

Michel Foucault has emerged as one of the most influential thinkers of the twentieth century. All of his analyses concern the modern organization of theoretical and practical knowledge and its relation to forms of social organization. Foucault carries out each of his analyses through a specific case study; Cousins and Hussain structure their examination around a faithful exposition of those principal case histories. Their excursion provides an invaluable guide through Foucault's labyrinth.

1984	*278 pp.*	*0-312-53166-4*	*$27.95 (cloth)*
		0-312-53167-2	*$11.95 (paper)*

Available at a 30% academic discount from

St. Martin's Press
Scholarly and Reference Books
175 Fifth Avenue • New York, NY 10010

CONTRIBUTORS

Authors

LUDWIG BINSWANGER (1881-1966) was born in Kreuzlingen, Switzerland and took his medical degree at the University of Zurich in 1907, and worked with C. G. Jung and Eugen Bleuler. In 1911 he became Chief Medical Director of the Bellevue Sanatorium in Kreuzlingen. It was Jung who introduced Binswanger to Freud, resulting in a lengthy friendship (recorded in Binswanger's *Sigmund Freud: Reminiscences of a Friendship*, 1957). Binswanger's brand of psychoanalysis was strongly influenced by his understanding of Heidegger's *Being and Time* (1927), culminating in what Binswanger called "existential analysis" (*Daseinsanalyse*). The essay "Dream and Existence" (1930) was Binswanger's first undertaking of this new existential analysis. Basically, he argued for a less reductionistic model for psychiatry than the natural scientific one, and for the use of the phenomenological method. He authored, among others, *On the Flight of Ideas* (1933), *Selected Lectures and Addresses* (1942-55, 2 vols.), *Schizophrenia* (1957), and *Melancholy and Mania* (1960). His works have appeared in English translation in Rollo May's *Existence* (1958), (most notably "The Case of Ellen West") and Jacob Needleman's collection *Being-in-the-World: Selected Papers of Ludwig Binswanger* (1963).

MICHEL FOUCAULT (1926-1984) was born in Poitiers, France and studied at the École Normal Supérieure in Paris, where he received his *licence* in philosophy in 1948, and in psychology in 1950, and his Diplôme de Psycho-Pathologie in 1952. Between 1952 and 1954 he taught at the École Normal and observed psychiatric practice in Parisian mental hospitals. In 1954 he published a lengthy introduction to an article by the Swiss existential psychiatrist Ludwig Binswanger, as well as his first book, *Mental Illness and Psychology*. In 1959, he received his *doctorat d'etat*, the highest degree awarded in France, in the history of science. In 1961 his doctoral thesis, *Madness and Civilization* was published in France, earning the Medal of the Centre de la Recherche Scientifique. In 1963 he published *The Birth of the Clinic*, followed by *The Order of Things* (1966), *Discipline and Punish* (1975), and his last works on *The History of Sexuality* (1976), a projected six volume set. He lectured and taught at various universities, and held the title of Professor of History of Systems of Thought at the Collège de France.

Translators

JACOB NEEDLEMAN is Professor of Philosophy, San Francisco State University. He is the editor and translator of *Being-in-the-World: Selected Papers of Ludwig Binswanger*, and author of *The New Religions, A Sense of the Cosmos, Lost Christianity, The Way of the Physician, Consciousness and the Tradition*, and *The Heart of Philosophy*.

FORREST WILLIAMS is Professor of Philosophy, University of Colorado, Boulder. He is the translator of Jean-Paul Sartre's *Imagination: A Psychological Critique* and *The Transcendence of the Ego*, as well as works by Gaston Bachelard, Gabriel Marcel, Maurice Merleau-Ponty, and Paul Ricoeur. He is also the author of numerous articles, including "The Mystique of Unconscious Creation," (in *Creativity and Learning*) and "Maurice Merleau-Ponty" (in *France in North America*).

Studies in Phenomenology and Existential Philosophy:

■ Jacques Derrida
Speech and Phenomena and Other Essays on Husserl's Theory of Signs
while evaluating Husserl, is, in its own right, an important analytical
work in the philosophy of language.

166 pp.   cloth $21.95
                                             paper $9.95

■ Emmanuel Levinas
The Theory of Intuition in Husserl's Phenomenology
philosophizes with Husserl rather than about him, treating intuition
as philosophical self-reflection.

165 pp.   cloth $25.95
                                    now in paper $10.95

■ Maurice Merleau-Ponty
The Primacy of Perception
takes up the major themes of Merleau-Ponty's work on perception.

256 pp.   cloth $21.95
                                             paper $8.95

■ Jean-Paul Sartre
The Writings of Jean-Paul Sartre: Selected Prose
spans the years 1923-64 in thirty-two short pieces including Sartre's
first play.

264 pp.   cloth $21.95
                                    now in paper $10.95

■ Herbert Spiegelberg
Phenomenology in Psychology and Psychiatry
in studying the relationships between disciplines, is an important
contribution to the history of ideas.

411 pp.   cloth $25.95
                                             paper $13.95

(For a complete list of titles in this series, write or call for a catalogue.)

Northwestern University Press

Related books of interest:

■ **Roland Barthes**
Critical Essays
is made up of 34 essays tracing the author's conversion to structuralism.
290 pp.   paper $10.95

■ **Arnold Hauser**
The Philosophy of Art History
is concerned with the methodology of art history, and, therefore, with
questions about historical thinking.
440 pp.   paper $13.95

■ **Michael Holquist**
Dostoevsky and the Novel
provides detailed readings of major works with reference to
Dostevsky's personal and moral preoccupations.
207 pp.   paper $9.95

■ **Charles Newman**
The Post-Modern Aura: The Act of Fiction in an Age of Inflation
evaluates the "post-modern" orientation in modern fiction.
205 pp.   paper $9.95

■ **Marjorie Perloff**
The Poetics of Indeterminacy: Rimbaud to Cage
studies an alternative tradition in recent literary history, examining
the uses of indeterminacy and chance in art.
466 pp.   paper $14.95

■ **Alain Robbe-Grillet**
Snapshots
is a collection of brilliant short pieces invaluable in their own right,
important in introducing readers to the work of the innovative stylist.
72 pp.   paper $6.95

Northwestern University Press
1735 Benson Avenue ◊ Evanston, Illinois 60201 ◊ (312) 491-5313

Northwestern University Press

Gardner Press — Selected Titles

New **ON BEING A PSYCHOTHERAPIST: The Journey of the Healer**
Carl Goldberg, Ph.D. Foreword by James Grotstein, M.D.
"The range of Dr. Goldberg's perspective is awesome."—James Grotstein
In this compassionate and revealing exploration of the personal and professional effects of therapeutic practice, the author provides an in-depth purview of the person of the practitioner.   ISBN 0-89876-112-3   392 pp.

EXISTENTIAL PSYCHOTHERAPY: The Process of Caring *David G. Edwards, M.S.W., Ph.D.*
Addressed to anyone involved in the therapeutic endeavor, this vital work reveals the existential character of caring and its integral place in the therapeutic process.
ISBN 0-89876-007-0   154 pp.

Forthcoming **PSYCHOLOGICAL TIME AND MENTAL ILLNESS** *Matthew Edlund, M.D.* As exciting and multifaceted as any aspect of human behavior, the study of time merits greater emphasis. Dr. Edlund's book is an attempt to explore the myriad ways in which it can be used to advantage in therapy and clinical practice.   ISBN 0-89876-122-0   128 pp.

THE YEARBOOK OF PSYCHOANALYSIS AND PSYCHOTHERAPY Volume 2/1986 *Edited by Robert Langs, M.D.* The contributors to this volume represent a wide range of background and orientation. Taken as a whole, the book offers a unique multidisciplinary perspective on many of the most significant clinical issues relevant to today's practitioner. ISBN 0-89876-141-7   approx. 256 pp.

PRIMER IN PSYCHOTHERAPY *Robert Langs, M.D.* Offering a concise review of established precepts in our understanding of basic mental functioning, as well as new insights into the nature of therapeutic interaction, Dr. Langs provides the tools necessary to participate in effective clinical work.   ISBN 0-89876-142-5   approx. 220 pp.

Send for your free Gardner Press Catalog.
Gardner Press, Inc., 19 Union Square West, New York, NY 10003

"A distinguished volume, a major book on the topic,
and of amazingly high quality."
—J. Hillis Miller

Reconstructing Individualism
Autonomy, Individuality, and the Self in
Western Thought

Edited by Thomas C. Heller, Morton Sosna, and David E. Wellbery,
with Arnold I. Davidson, Ann Swidler, and Ian Watt. The 16 distinguished essays collected in this volume display a wide diversity in their views of individualism that is altogether appropriate to the complexity of the theme and the eight disciplines represented by the contributors. The contributors are: Christine Brooke-Rose, Stanley Cavell, Nancy Julia Chodorow, James Clifford, Natalie Zemon Davis, John Freccero, Michael Fried, Carol Gilligan, Stephen Greenblatt, Ian Hacking, Werner Hamacher, Niklas Luhmann, John W. Meyer, Martha C. Nussbaum, J. B. Schneewind, and Paolo Valesio. Cloth, $39.50; paper, $11.95

 **Stanford University Press**
STANFORD, CA 94305

SUNY Press

Available in November

Dream Life, Wake Life by Gordon G. Globus

"*Dream Life, Wake Life* presents an original, clearly explained theory of dreams and associated mental mechanisms that is based on a broad interdisciplinary background, including phenomenology, analytical philosophy, psychoanalysis, and contemporary cognitive psychology." — Quentin Smith

Dream Life, Wake Life addresses human creativity as illuminated by dreaming. While Freud held a "transformative" view of dreaming in which dream life is secondhand, formed by combining memory traces of diverse past waking experiences into novel compositions; Gordon Globus sees the process as creative, the fundamental creative action inherent in the human condition. 192 pp. (tent.) $10.95 pb.

Also of interest
Beyond the Brain: *Birth, Death, and Transcendence in Psychotherapy* by Stanislav Grof. 256 pp. $12.95 pb.

State University Plaza • Albany, NY 12246

New from Duke

Polanyian Meditations
In Search of a Post-Critical Logic
William H. Poteat
1985. x, 330 pages, $39.50

Bodily Reflective Modes
A Phenomenological Method for Psychology
Kenneth Joel Shapiro
Foreword by Amedeo Giorgi
1984. xxi, 230 pages, $30

Forthcoming in 1987

The Ecology of the Body
Joseph Lyons

Duke University Press
6697 College Station   Durham, North Carolina 27708

Review of Existential Psychology & Psychiatry

Vol. XIX   No. 1

DREAM & EXISTENCE

Michel Foucault & Ludwig Binswanger

Translated by
Forrest Williams & Jacob Needleman

Publication of this special issue was aided by a grant from the Publications Program of the National Endowment for the Humanities, an independent federal agency.

Vol. XIX, Nos. 2 & 3

Includes original articles on Freud & Sartre, Kierkegaard & therapy, Medard Boss, rational-emotive therapy, a phenomenology of pain, and other topics.

Special Forthcoming Issue
MICHEL FOUCAULT'S ARCHAEOLOGY OF PSYCHIATRY

ORDER FORM

	Individuals	Institutions
_____ *Dream & Existence* Issue Only (Vol. XIX, No. 1)	$10	$20
_____ Regular U.S. Subscription (Vol. XIX, Nos. 1, 2, 3)	$20	$40

(Foreign Subscriptions, please add $3/Vol. for postage)

Enclosed is my check/purchase order (payable to REPP) for $ _____.

Name _____

Address_____

City_____State_____Zip_____

Address all correspondence to: Keith Hoeller, *Editor*
Review of Existential Psychology & Psychiatry
P.O. Box 23220, Seattle, WA 98102

Special Issue Forthcoming in the *Review*

MICHEL FOUCAULT'S ARCHAEOLOGY
OF PSYCHIATRY

ISBN 0-914857-03-7

Information for subscribers is listed
on the inside back cover.